The Penalties
for Not Being a
Lady First

A Guide to What Men & Women
are Looking for in Each Other

Anthony "TJ" Jamison

The Penalties

for Not Being a

Lady First

A Guide to What Men & Women
are Looking for in Each Other

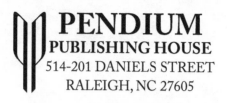

PENDIUM
PUBLISHING HOUSE
514-201 DANIELS STREET
RALEIGH, NC 27605

For information, please visit our Web site at
www.pendiumpublishing.com

PENDIUM Publishing and its logo
are registered trademarks.

The Penalties for Not Being A Lady First
by Anthony "TJ" Jamison

Copyright © Anthony "TJ" Jamison, 2019
All Rights Reserved.

ISBN: 978-1-944348-98-4

SPECIAL THANKS

None of this would be possible without my mother and father, Rosa Mae and James Rudolph Jamison. Thanks for everything. I love you guys to life.

To my brothers and sisters, we made it out of that concrete jungle safe and in our right minds.

To my wife, the wind beneath my wings. To my four boys, Galen, Travon, Gene, and Anthony: you are part of my inspiration.

To my dear spiritual leaders, the (late) Dr. Frank and JoNell Summerfield: you have truly been a lamp to my feet.

And to everyone who touched my life in any way... Thank you!

Bookings

Author, Entrepreneur, Counselor,

Motivational Speaker, Inspiring Inventor

Call 919.805.8603 or Email bookings@tjjamison.com

Anthony "TJ" Jamison

PREFACE

There's two things I learned about in this life, and they never fail to come through on their promises. Women and fires will both kill you if they get out of control. One of the things I have discovered is if you want your woman to follow you, you must give her a clear path to where you're going together as a family. Individuals in relationships must see and have a clear vision of the future for things to work out. Women, in my opinion, are stronger than dirt by themselves, but with spouses they become SUPERWOMEN! *(Women, in some ways are like tea bags: you'll never know how strong they really are until you put them in hot water).* In my writings, one of the things I'm trying to convey to men and women is everything that we're looking for is in each other, just like Eve was in Adam. Where she was strategically placed was the most. Nobody but God would've thought of such a place to put the rib right under the man's armpit at his side, not behind him, over or under him but at his side to rule together with him side by side. His arm protects her, and the ribcage protects all his vital organs of the body such as the heart, lungs, and liver that are needed to keep living. I wonder if he knew that she kept and keeps us alive.

Let me give you an overview of the hardest working person alive today: the woman. The woman houses our

favor in Proverbs 18:22. Also in that same book she is known as *wisdom*, while in 1 Peter 3:7, she determines if our prayers are hindered by God. Ladies and gentlemen, the women we know as ladies are nothing short of amazing. Proverbs 31:10 tells us that *"her worth is far above rubies."* Gentlemen, if you don't have a woman, let me recommend something to you: find one immediately! And watch your life change because she was made to help you win in every area of life. My goal in this writing is to help mankind to know we are not only built to last, but made to love, honor, and respect one another. When God made us, He made us to live somewhere forever, whether we choose to live in heaven or hell it's final. So, since we're going to live forever somewhere, it might as well be with the KING of everything — God —and his leading lady, the Woman.

One of the hardest things to find today is love, or should I say *true love,* because honesty is such a lonely word. Until women come to the knowledge of their worth and men know women's value, relationships as a whole will keep taking a beating, to say the least. This book gives ladies the information, understanding, and skills to keep them from being penalized by the system of chauvinism.

Finding your soulmate and your passion is a beautiful thing, but unfortunately many do not know what a **diamond in the rough** looks like, etc.: (having exceptional qualities or potential but lacking refinement or polish) This is one of the biggest problems men have in relationships with women. One of greatest gifts God created and gave to man was the woman, hands down. The woman is the giver of life. She singlehandedly secured mankind's safe passage or place in history when she loaned her body to be used as the vehicle to carry and deliver the Savior of the world safely to us. If she can carry that type of **POWER**, one can only imagine what else she is capable of carrying in the rough. (That refinement place).

A powerful verse that changed my life concerning woman is Proverbs 18:22. *"A man that finds a wife, finds a good thing and obtains favor from the Lord."* The keyword is (favor.) Men, instead of trying to find favor with the boss, just find a wife and treat her right, and you will have INSTANT FAVOR! When I wrote this book, I had ladies mainly in mind, but the wisdom and intelligence that God used me to share in this writing are, by far, universal.

P.S. - It's documented in the Word of God, the hidden treasure of success is found in the woman and guess what? I found it."

CONTENTS

Chapter 1

Like A Butterfly: Pretty to See, But Hard to Catch

A woman should be like a butterfly: pretty to see but hard to catch. To catch a butterfly, you must first approach it slowly from behind so that you don't harm it or let it fly away. When I was growing up we use to catch Bees, in jar's as they were pollinating flowers, that was an easy catch. But because of the way butterflies, fly, up and down back and forth it's a hard catch.

The biblical book of Ruth is a beautiful story of love, loyalty, and redemption.

> **Ruth 1:16 (ESV)**
> **But Ruth said, "Do not urge me to leave you or to return from following you. For where you go I will go, and where you lodge I will lodge. Your people shall be my people, and your God my God.**

One of the only two books of the bible named after a woman, this Masterpiece tells the story of the salvation of Ruth the Moabite through her relationship with her mother-in-law Naomi, Ruth learned about the living

God and became his devoted follower. Abandoning her family and homeland, she demonstrated both her love for her widowed mother-in-law, and her faith in Israel's God. Her faith was well placed, for God not only provided for her, but He also helped her in the royal family line. Already, we can see God's hand all over Ruth's and Naomi's lives, and it was for one reason: love. Naomi was an exceptional woman of God, her commitment and love for God attracted Ruth.

In Psalm 8:5, the psalmist poses the question.
"what is man that God is so mindful of him and made him just a little lower than the angels."

It's his love. When we follow God's plan, he will always make a way for us. In Ruth's story, Ruth and her mother-in-law were not only widowed, but down on their luck, also. And the last thing they needed in their lives was an ungodly man bringing them down. So, God put his Masterful handprint all over **Ruth and Naomi.** Women of God, don't you ever think you need to settle for less than what God said about you. He has a plan for your life if you remain faithful to his will and his way. God's type of love is a genuine love that keeps its promises. There's a valuable lesson to be learned, not just for women, but for mankind, because God responds to genuine love. For example, Ruth had no knowledge of Naomi's God **yet**, but had such genuine love for her mother-in-law that she was willing to leave what she knew and move to Naomi's world, which was for Ruth, the unknown. Her keen sense of loyalty moved her to a place of royalty, protection, and being provided for. This is God's plan for his greatest *Masterpiece:* woman. In this case, God's providential hand redeemed Ruth and Naomi from poverty. It's evident He controlled circumstances so that **Ruth and Boaz** would meet. And He prompted Boaz to fulfill the responsibility of the kinsman redeemer. The kinsman was the defender of the family's rights. Women of God, I know you're saying I don't want my relative for my husband. *(Hello)*... I understand that; but it's not the family connection between Ruth and Boaz I want you to focus on. I want you to focus on how God makes ways out of no way if your focus stays on Him. So, women, be the butterfly and watch God prompt your Boaz to find you. Read what the bible says:

Proverbs 18:22 (ESV)
He who finds a wife finds a good thing
and obtains favor from the Lord.

That verse changes my whole life, gentlemen not only does a wife help you to win in life, she also houses your favor inside of her. FYI: That's even more reason for you to make love, searching for your favor with-in your spouse, Smile... A husband whose wife is like the woman described in Proverbs 31 should rejoice in her because her noble character brings him honor like a king. An excellent wife is the crown on her husband's head. So, ladies, you need to know that men aren't just looking for a good time. (Well, not all men.) There is something down in his soul that wants more. Oh yes, he clearly identifies with his penis contacting with your vagina, but his soul wants more. So, in most cases, a man will have sex with you and never see you again because his penis got satisfied, but his soul is still looking for much more. The bible says he who finds a wife obtains favor to be recognized, established, and endowed with special advantages or gifts, even preferential treatment. A man getting laid is none of those things. *(Do you understand, the words that are coming out of my mouth)?* Do you realize that you can get sex anywhere for free? And most men — most people, as far as that is concerned — never respect that which is free. So, if you are still trying to figure out why he doesn't love you after you gave yourself to him, it might be because you were successful in meeting his wants but failed at meeting his needs. So, you say, *(how do you know the difference, between wants and needs)?*

I'm glad you asked.

Look at it like this: wants can be met with flesh. On the other hand, needs pertain to life essentials like food, clothing, and shelter.

Philippians 4:19 shows us that God has a bigger picture of what we need.

Philippians 4:19 (ESV)
And my God will supply every need of yours
according to his riches in glory in Christ Jesus.

So even though He will give us the desires of our heart, He meets our every need. So, I think Ruth met the need of Boaz before he got what he wanted. Sometimes women today provide the wants and needs in reverse, so men end up being studs and women end up looking for love in all the wrong places.

In the days of old, a woman losing her virginity was a time for celebration, because it was God's way of doing things; it was the way God ordained new life to come into the world, with husband and wife's. Kids and family now are like recreational drugs; just for **fun**. No connection or relationship, just a **(big butt and a smile)**. And women, rarely men, are being penalized for not being ladies first. In Ruth 2:2, Ruth asked Naomi if she could go and glean in the farmer's field that she might find favor.

Ruth 2:2 (ESV)
And Ruth the Moabite said to Naomi,
"Let me go to the field and glean among the
ears of grain after him in whose sight
I shall find favor."

Here, Ruth is asking for work, an honest day's work. She is not saying let me go to the club and shake my booty. She put herself in a position to be cared for, not used and abused. Though Ruth did not intentionally go to the field of Boaz, it was the Lord who providentially directed and ordered her steps. My sister, you don't have to go looking for a man; just glean, *(work and move)* in the right places. Ruth made use of the stipulations the Lord gave Boaz. God had told Boaz to tell the young men not to harvest their field completely; instead, they were to leave some unharvested so that the poor and the strangers in the land could gather up food for their survival; Ruth was among them.

Boaz demonstrated extraordinary concern for Ruth's provision and protection. He even thought of Ruth's need for water in the heat of the day. Still today, men are looking for someone to care for and take home to Mama. To be the one who gets

God was looking out for us way before we needed Him. *That reminder was a freebie.*

to meet Mama, you just have to avoid the *penalties for not being a lady first.* Showing off your body to strangers is not a **turn-on**; in fact, it's a **turnoff**. Oh yeah, we men like the porn, but you won't meet Mama, and forget about wifey list, if you become a source of porn for a man. Have you ever noticed guys that have real girlfriends, just friends, strictly platonic relationships for a long time? Have you ever asked yourself, *"Why are they still friends?"* The reason why is she isn't giving him nothing. He hangs on because she is meeting his needs first, with her legs closed.

See, most men don't really want to have sex without a relationship. Oh, a man will take sex if it is available because some women give it up so fast. He doesn't have time to tell you what he really wants and needs… so he goes along with the program of sticking and moving; the game some women let men play. *Are you starting to see where I'm coming from?* I'm starting to think girls just want to have fun also. And I think you should, but not at the expense of your future! You must remember, emphasis on **must**, there's a penalty for not being a lady first; and it is **a price you can't afford, losing your respect.**

So, Ruth is not playing the field. She's gleaning in the field. The moment you give up your goods, you're off the wifey list. *Let's get something clear: it's not just about wifey. It's about integrity.*

I'll never forget a story my brother told me about first impressions. He said to me one day as I was making a deal with another young man buying a car, he said to me *"everything you want to happen in a deal, get it up front, because once the deal is made, it is what it is."* In other words, my brother was telling me that you get no more out of the original deal once it's made. For example:

When you buy a car and want free oil changes for the life of the car, get that guarantee up front and in writing because after you buy the car, the deal is done or dead. Ladies, the same goes for dating men. If you want him to bring you home to Mama one day, keep your panties on for as long as you can single. If you can't, please don't exchange semen, why? Because it's a deal breaker, I don't make the rules, but it is. That the one thing we save for the ONE! Look at all the single ladies with kids with no man, now answer that for yourself.

I know you just said, what is wrong with him talking like that? Nothing! It's the truth. If I can test drive a car every day, year in and year out, I don't care how much I like that car, I ain't buying it — at least not that one. ... Unless you sell it to me cheap or at half price. Now this is where the fight begins. After you use and abuse me with all your rental abuse, driving me all around town, hitting the curb and riding the rail and hitting the bottom, you won't buy the car unless I sell it for cheap. Well this is one of the penalties for not being a lady first; being **underappreciated.** The definition of depreciation is to deduct from taxable income a portion of the original cost of a business asset over several years as the value of the asset decreases to grow progressively less. Remember I said, *"the more you give of yourself, the more you lose of you"*. That's just what happens when you lose your **advantage**, and women all over the world are losing the advantage; throwing in your trump card too soon.

You know when you're playing cards, you hold your best cards to beat your opponent's best cards, but if you throw your best cards in too soon, you lose, and women are losing when it comes to men and relationships; giving up their **best too soon**. Oh, but not Ruth, she's gleaning.

Look how the prophet Isaiah used this word to describe how the Lord would gather up his people from among all the nations and restore them to their own land.

Isaiah 27:12 (ESV)
**and you will be gleaned one by one, O people
of Israel.**

If we as people would hold on to God's ways not just women, but all of us, the way we hold on to tips in *(salon and restaurant)*, He would not only gather us back to Him, He would restore all... Everything that the enemy stole. I think the thing that moved God the most about Ruth was a short verse in the first chapter of Ruth, verse 16, when she said, *"Your people shall be my people and your God, my God."* I believe God just got all mushy inside about her loving on Him on just words from her mother-in-law. That's huge.

Ruth 1:16 (ESV)
**Your people shall be my people,
and your God my God.**

This is another type of gleaning — to get or gather information or material bit by bit. I don't believe Ruth knew Boaz that well, but I believe she got enough information on him to know who to reap after. (That will preach) ... Woman of God, if you don't do anything else right in life, associate with people who have a charge to keep and a God to glorify. Ruth followed people who had a God conscience. When she said, "Let me go in the field and glean after him." Who was he? ...and whose sight I may find favor. Ladies who are the (hims) that you are following? Ruth is following not just a man of great wealth, but a person of noble character and of high standing. Simply put, a Boaz, not a *jackass.*

In the original nursery rhyme, Jack and Jill went up the hill "to fetch a pail of water." The 1970s musical group Raydio changed the story so that Jack went down the hill because he needed love that he couldn't get from Jill. (YouTube Raydio's song "Jack and Jill."). Jack represents the kind of man who is always up to no good. If the man you think you are meant to be with is with someone else, you don't need him. So, glean after *God's man.* Don't just go after him; Glean with him and prove yourself to be what God made you to be: *man's better half.*

Let's back up just for a moment. Ruth said "please, let me glean after the reapers." Now, let all of us learn from this woman. She didn't want to be put out front before her time; she took the low road, not the less of; but humbled herself and God exalted her in more ways than one. He blessed her exceedingly and abundantly and all she did was glean. She didn't have to play house, make babies, or lose her integrity or self-respect. *All she did was glean.*

The penalties for not being a lady first will cause you to lose not only your reputation in the community, but also your Boaz. Ruth gleaned from behind, all the way to meal time; where she sat right beside the reapers. This is just how God hooks his people up. Ruth started out in the back, but she ended up sitting right beside the help. As musician Drake proclaims, she *"started from the bottom now [she's] here!"* When we follow God's plan, He causes us to triumph all the time. When we revisit the word of God, marriage was God's response to the first thing in creation that He called not good (Genesis

2:18). So, all a woman really needs to do to get a man in accordance with this scripture is be a **lady.**

Genesis 2:18 (ESV)
Then the Lord God said, "It is not good that
the man should be alone;

God did not want Adam or man to be lonely, so He fashioned a helper comparable to him. Adam and his helper were similar; alike. When the woman is something like man, she is now truly fitting and fully adequate for her God-given helper. Because most men don't know what they're really looking for, some will just grab the first thing shaking. Not only does the woman have to walk upright, she should do double duty and show him the way also. *Talk about a double standard!*

Please don't get mad at me. I'm just reporting the news. The penalty for not being a lady first has so many setbacks with God and man. Think about *fornication.* Most, if not all, men want to test drive the car before they buy it, I know I do, just kidding. Smile…. Test driving a car before you buy it, that's the only way to purchase a car, but to test drive you its fornication, fake marriage if there's such a thing. Now there was a time when we used to kick the tires, look under the hood, and check the brakes. **No more.** Now, we walk around the car, pump the brakes and drive the hell out of it! It is no longer enough to cruise around to check the car out; we want to hit the gas and spin out of the parking lot. We want to dip our sticks everywhere and check the oil, and not just the motor oil. Now we want to check all the oils, the transmission fluid, and the brake fluid. In other words, we want to dip our stick in the front and in the back.

Now what response goes here: *(Hello or Hell to the no)?* Let me tell you something, ladies. When you let anybody do all that to you, he ain't even test driving anymore. You just became a **test dummy** and you know what test dummies are used for. Yes, that's right, to get things right for the real thing: *the other woman.*

Fornication has a negative effect on your self-image and taints our relationship with God and man. People forget that once we come to know Christ, our bodies become the temple of God where the Holy Spirit lives. You just can't let people go in and out of your house. That goes for your spiritual dwelling as well as your natural home. That's crazy. When I lived in the projects growing up, people just didn't come in and out of my mother's house. You could get hurt. I'm not talking spiritually, but physically -- *like oops upside the head.* And that's just what's happening to women today, because men are not keeping their **promise.** Even though there's a penalty for not being a lady first, look who's losing out: all of us. Our kids are fatherless, our fathers are childless, and our women have no husbands. *Remember the saying, mama's baby daddy's maybe?*

Well that holds true, and on top of that there's no family structure or guidance. In my first book, I stated that *"a child without a father, is like an explorer without a compass".* Remember **Jacques Cousteau?** He was a great explorer who sailed the seven seas a french oceanographer, researcher, filmmaker, and undersea explorer. He was arguably the most famous undersea explorer of modern times and all he had outside of his crew sometimes was a *compass.* Today we have *navigation systems,* those little devices that help mankind get around the world. Just like the compass, you don't need directions on paper because you have that device to lead and guide you. That's what fathers do for children: give them supervision, lead them into acceptable conduct, and guide them by pointing out the proper route to follow in life. Mothers have been doing it forever, but it's Dads job.

A child without this type of device, known as dad, to guide him or her could be lost. I wish I had the chance to fix my relationships with some of my kids, all of them are good kids I was just never there to show them the right ways, so you tell me who's really getting screwed? If I lost my way in life, the first thing I would do is go back to the old landmark, Mom and Dad. My brothers and sisters, we must go back to the beginning, the old landmark, because we're not just hurting ourselves, we're hurting the babies, and that's a no-no. When Boaz favored Ruth, he was paying attention to detail and his surroundings. He was well aware of who was prepared and who was not. We've all made bad choices in the past, but you can now begin to glean in the right places to make yourself marketable. The Boazes of this world are looking for their Ruth's and they want their Ruth's to be prepared, mainly because for each Boaz, his Ruth is his gift into the favor of God.

I don't want to sound old fashioned, but the word of God says, *"he who finds a wife finds a good thing."* Now before I go any further with this good thing, does the scripture say *he* that finds or *she* that finds? I'm just checking, because this could be a big part of our problem with mankind. We have gotten the he and the she mixed up.

Back to what men are looking for... a man is looking for his favor. Some of the problems in marriage today arise from a breakdown in communication of mutual respect, not from some flaw in marriage itself. In other words, when a man finds his wife, the blessings of the Lord begin to flow in the couple's lives. That's what most men are looking for: a steady flow of blessings and trust between two people. Lots of men are very successful by themselves, but something is missing. Oh yeah, God's favor is missing. People of God, we need to realize that we are living in a world that promotes a double standard about promiscuity, that double standard is just as prevalent in the church as it is in the world.

Men with multiple sex partners are **dashing and hip,** women on the other hand are seen as **loose and whorish**. We all know these stereotypes are wrong either way! But no man or woman wants a whore, at least not in public! I know that sucks, but it's the truth. I said in public because we do some funky stuff behind closed doors. *Yes, we do. All of us.* We love to use and abuse, because once a man has his way with you, you just killed the glean he once saw in you. And now he's on his way looking for *Miss Right,* and he's going through and past you to get to her. Hello!

So, woman seeking God, when a member of the male species comes to you out of order, you must put him in check. You must call him on his disrespect and let him know he must have you mixed up with someone else. Flirting is exciting; but flirtation will get you a temporary fix, but no Boaz. Remember the woman caught in the act of adultery? The way the writer describes the scene, it was like the woman was by herself. If she was caught, who in the *(ham sandwich)* was she caught with? That's the double standard. The word of God said she was caught in the very act. How was she caught, but not the man? If we could get one thing out of this text it would be, if he's *"nachos"* (not yours), tell him to dip and stop letting him take a dip. ... When a man starts to flirt with you, most, not all, are setting you up for hugs and kisses. My barber calls kissing *"uptown shopping for downtown business."* The penalties for not being a lady first will cost you everything. At least it did for David and Bathsheba.

There are two principal scriptures I want to dissect, first the apostle Paul warns us in 1 Corinthians 6:18 to flee from sexual immorality.

1 Corinthians 6:18 (ESV)
Flee from sexual immorality.

We should really look closely at this text because it goes straight to the point I am trying to make. Flee. You can't get any clearer than that. Fornication is something singles deal with; committing adultery is something married people deal with. One thing is clear, then: if you find yourself in a situation in which you are in danger of committing *fornication or adultery,* the bible says Run! It said flee, but I gave you the Elder. Jamison version... yours truly. Smile...

People of God, this sin is the big one, because it is one that is committed against the place — the house, the temple — where the **Holy Spirit dwells**. This sin is against yourself as well as the Holy Spirit. The thought of sexual sin is almost as bad as the act. It brought Joseph from overseer of Potiphar's commercial, professional, and public affairs to a prisoner... just the thought. At least that's what Potiphar's wife said about him, (we know she lied). This is the same thing happening to men and women today all over the world. We're losing our positions because of sexual sin (lies from the devil). The price Jesus paid was for all of us not just to save us, but to cleanse us from all unrighteousness. Sin is bondage like slavery, and Jesus's death paid for us in full to be redeemed from bondage to all sin.

Luke 10:19 (ESV)
Behold, I have given you authority to tread on serpents and scorpions, and over all the power of the enemy, and nothing shall hurt you.

The temple in this text is the place where the Holy Spirit lives. In my opinion, this is a crucial point that we all miss. Paul told all believers that each one of our bodies is a sanctuary for God, just like the church is a spiritual temple for God's people. Now the glory of God and the person of the Holy Spirit dwells within every believer. This is where the penalty for not being a lady first is huge in sexual sin. The thing a man leaves in a woman after sex, (semen) is *polluting every fiber of her being.* This is how the woman got caught in the very act of adultery she was stuck with guilt and shame. The man just looked at the sex act as if he just went to the restroom. For him, the sex was just nature taking its course. He moved on from the woman who provided him temporary relief. *(Looking at what you did from this perspective might make you want to hurt him. Don't hurt him, just stop giving yourself away.)* The woman, on the other hand, is left with all the spirits he slept with that week, month, and year. She is drained of her strength daily. Instead of the woman gleaning, she is now feigning like a junkie for drugs. She is now fighting thousands of demons that were left inside her through sexual sin. **Sexual sin** is something like AIDS HIV, and EBOLA as dangerous and life threatening as it is, you can still live with it, *but it's killing little parts of you every day.*

The next scripture I would like to open is 2 Samuel 11, which confirms that sexual sin is a death trap. It caused David to shed innocent blood. Read the letter he sent by Uriah, to the messenger.

2 Samuel 11:15 (ESV)
In the letter he wrote, "Set Uriah in the forefront of the hardest fighting, and then draw back from him, that he may be struck down, and die."

If you look at this text like most people, you would say David was wrong: for sleeping with his servant's wife and move on from there; but in this case, sexual sin played more of a role when it came to life and death. Sex is God's way of unifying husband and wife in this world, but sexual sin has a way of taking life out of this world. Like we saw with David and Bathsheba and her husband Uriah, sexual sin is happening all over the world. While it may not lead to physical death, it certainly contributes to spiritual death. The penalty for not being a lady first causes men to use their power to deceive friend and foe.

If David was out in the battle like his men, we could say maybe this horrible thing would not have happened. But because he stayed behind, an innocent man died. I don't want to put the blame on Bathsheba, but I want women to look closely at the power they possess, especially when it comes to men. Men were created to worship God but made to care for women. David wanted that woman so badly that he killed for her; and if you know it or not, he'll do the same for you; maybe not kill physically but will do almost anything outside of that. You don't have to undress before your time, because if he wants you badly enough, he'll *"put a ring on it" first...* at least that's what Beyoncé said. That is, if he really wants you. It's that simple. Glean and be about your father's business and watch all the real looks you get. Not the bathroom eyes full of doo-doo, but the looks that go with applications for you to become a future wife.

There's something everybody wants, but nobody is getting. It's like a virgin; they are hard to find over a certain age, like in the teens. People of God that to soon! I hope I did not overshoot. All you must do as a woman wanting a man is be yourself. *We love difference.* Nobody can be a better you than you. When I think about what a man wants in a woman, I think about the Proverbs 31 woman and all she brings to the table. Who can find a virtuous woman, the tasks that involve her life, the resources, her independence, and acts for the families; her consideration for others and the way her reputation makes her husband look good. That's a turn-on all by itself; and she's fully dressed. She's dressed in strength and honor. Women trust me on this: every man is looking for this woman and wants to know what's under her **hood;** and what's in her **head.** And all she's doing is being herself; no nightclub, no booty shorts, no twerking, and definitely no test driving. She's focused and clear in her intentions.

She speaks wisdom and she never misuse words. **Yes, is yes. No is no.** No lead-on's. No room for mistakes. The virtuous woman is blessed. Her children love her as well as her husband. That's all great, but if I had one thing to celebrate about this woman, it would be that she fears the Lord, she reverences God and walks in His will. If I had one thing to tell women today, I would have to say, *a man adores a woman who fears the Lord.* That's how you glean: be pretty to see, but hard to catch, because nothing — I mean absolutely nothing — can replace a lady.

Chapter 2

The More You Give of Yourself
The More You Lose of You

John 4:7 (ESV)
A woman from Samaria came to draw water.
Jesus said to her, "Give me a drink."

I don't know what I like most about this bible story: the woman coming to draw water, or Jesus needing to go through Samaria. Either way, I see Jesus coming to the rescue, once again, of a lost soul. After all, the Jews had no dealings with Samaritans. Thank God that Jesus was not biased in that regard. This woman needed help and Jesus was the answer. When this woman came to draw water, little did she know Jesus would stop all the hurt and pain she once endured with strange men. After all, this woman had *five husbands,* and the one she was with when she encountered Jesus was not hers, either. So, if I'm counting right, this woman had six men in and out of her life. This is where our biggest problem comes in when it comes to dating and relationships: *spreading ourselves too thin.* One of the first things I noticed about this woman is that she is not named in the text. Other Jews wouldn't even speak with her. Not only do we have a loose woman, but we have a no-name woman as well. Even though people weren't speaking to this woman, Jesus was out to get to know her and heal her sin-sick soul. The first thing Jesus did was connect with her about a familiar interest (water). He established common ground. This common ground allowed Jesus to talk with her about her real issues (men). I think most men would be maximizing on what they perceived to be her real issue (sex). But Jesus is out to help her.

I would like to go on the record and say low self-esteem may have been the real culprit in this case. Low self-esteem has a way of causing people to do things they would not normally do. Low self-esteem is like drugs or alcohol; it causes you to show your weaker side. The sad part about it for any woman is that the *(more you give of yourself, the more you lose of you)*. In Bible days, women caught in sexual sin would be stoned. So, there was something more going on than just a good time. I think she may have been a harlot. Nevertheless, Jesus came to save her. The Samaritan woman said to Jesus, "How is it you ask drink of me?" because the Samaritans and Jews did not interact with each other. This tradition of separation lets us know this woman's own race of people was prostituting her because they had no dealings outside their race. The men she was with were Samaritans who were pimping her. Jesus aroused her interest and built a verbal bridge by making her thirsty for something more than H2O. He offered her *living water,* the *(Holy Spirit)* so she would never thirst again.

I'm not letting men off the hook for their meat locker mentality abusing women, but I need women to see and understand the blessings they forfeit for not being ladies first. Worse still, it's your own race of people that are abusing you the (men). Where do you go for help when home is abusing you? So, Jesus said He *had or needed to go through Samaria.* Therefore, I said "hold on" because sooner or later Jesus will show up and make everything all right. When Jesus said He needed to go, there must have been a *physiological* or *psychological deficiency* in this woman. Even though no one else neither saw nor cared, Jesus was on the way to give her living water. This woman was given more than she could afford to give of herself, so Jesus was on the way again to let her know He already paid it all, so she didn't have to give herself away, not even to the one man she had then, who was not her husband. When we think of this woman's mindset, we can only think of the pain she had to be going through. As soon as Jesus said, *"the one you have now is not yours,"* she said, *"in that you speak truly."* She totally surrendered, as if she was looking for a way out. Oh, bless his name! Right there, she surrendered her sinful life to Jesus.

Jesus, the Rock in a weary land, showed up not just as *King of Kings,* but as doctor and lawyer, as well. He first pleaded her case to God as a victim of the injustice of abusive men, then He healed her pain and let downs and disappointments from five divorces and a bad case of low self-esteem. This woman's pain had to be crippling, because she didn't even put up a fight or try to defend her decision to have all those men in and out of her life. Most people, when their hands are caught in the cookie jar have an excuse, but she said to Jesus, *"in that you speak truly,"* as if she needed someone to help her out of that fornicating, adulterous lifestyle.

I believe women today are looking for a way out of the life of catering to abusive men and dealing with broken promises. When people don't come through on promises, it hurts. The average woman today is disappointed and let down by the one person she is supposed to trust in. Just like the boy who cried wolf, she just does not believe in men anymore, and that's sad. So now, the heartbroken woman may just sleep around just like the men she used to believe in.

There are penalties for not being a lady first, and we must keep that in mind. One of the major penalties outside of your God-given blessing and prosperity is your **self-respect**. That alone should stop all the madness when it comes to men running in and out of your life. It should be come and stay or go and never come back. (Can I get some help up in here?)

I had a similar situation with a girlfriend. She thought she could walk in and out of my life, because she had the goods —*you know: the goods. Smile...* But I said you may come in, and you may walk out, but you will not be walking in and out of my life. She walked out with all the goods and has been trying ever since to get back. Still today, she's following me on *Facebook, Twitter, and Instagram* trying to be my friend socially.... Well I ain't no dummy; (excuse my bad grammar) she doesn't want to be my friend, she wants to walk back into my life. But the door is closed, and I have moved on. Notice: that I said the door is closed, not locked; because if it's locked, you can't come in and I can't go out. Don't let anyone incarcerate you. That door is just closed to her, I can go in and out and move on with my life, because people don't miss their water until their wells run dry. Ladies, if you're ever going to get the respect you deserve from men, you must put two things down: your foot and your dress. The only thing men respect outside of the law sometimes, is a woman holding out on him. *(And that*

34

isn't right, just so you know.) Women, that's your *weapon of mass destruction* to men: like Superman's weakness in the presence of kryptonite, your commitment to holding out will bring him to his knees. To a crawl and beg.

Hosea 4:6 (ESV)
My people are destroyed for lack of knowledge;

What I'm about to say to you now cost me everything. Our world does not teach two things intentionally that we need to survive in life: **#1, relationships** and **#2, economics;** because there's too much to gain on the back end, if you're in a servitude position (incarcerate, poor) there's lots of money to make off retraining you, and you know we perish for lack of knowledge.

We cannot afford to lose families or money; so, we must get it right now; so, Jesus is on his way to help the water fetcher. In our text, Jesus offered the nameless woman everlasting water, and the woman said, *"sir give me this water."* I don't know what this woman's initial intention was when she accepted Jesus's offer of living water since she had five husbands and a bad reputation all around town; nevertheless, she found an eternal love. Can you believe that after five men — that we know of — letting her down, she would try Jesus — another man. Thank God that, for her sake, Jesus was a man of his word. This woman, like many women today, was looking for a man just to keep his **word**. What's so hard about that? The woman tried again, like most women trying one more bad guy; just like the Samaritan, looking for love in all the wrong places. It's time to stop drinking the **devil's nectar** and drink from the *river of life*, Gods unfailing source: Jesus and his ever-flowing stream of living water.

Another penalty for not being a lady first is investing in ungodly men. It's a dangerous thing to love a man who doesn't love God. Most people need someone to be accountable to. When people don't have anyone to answer to, they *don't*. That's what you get when you link up with an ungodly person. The Bible calls being in such a relationship being *unequally yoked*. To be unequally yoked with someone, plain and simple, is like trying to mix oil and vinegar; they only mix well when they are shaken up together. Who wants to be shaken up all the time or mad to get along? Not me. That's what being unequally yoked is like: you are mad all the time and *shaken up*.

2 Corinthians 6:14 (ESV)
The Temple of the Living God do not be
unequally yoked with unbelievers.

I believe Jesus had a vested interest in the Samaritan woman and wanted to help her out of the penalties of being unequally yoked. Now, a yoke is good when two people are working together like oxen — joined at the neck, working together plowing a field. When your yoke is unequal, you're not working together, and that's another penalty for not being a lady first. You get yoked up with someone who has someone or something else in mind. It's hard enough being in a relationship with someone when you're on the same page. Simply stated, when you marry or hook up with an unbeliever, you are unequally yoked. In the world, that arrangement may seem okay, but when God is your father and you are yoked up with Jesus, and your spouse is yoked up with his father the devil, problems will come in. Now we see why Jesus said He **had** to go to Samaria. This woman must have been His daughter spiritually; maybe she was temporarily insane giving more than she had to give. Like most women, she must have found herself giving more than their share.

Instead of getting stronger, she was getting weaker. Jesus came to her rescue with living water. I'm so glad He didn't show up with food or money, because most working men have food and money. Instead, He showed up with life-sustaining help: something to fill the broken places in her life, something to stop the self-inflicted hurts that are associated with low self-esteem. This woman didn't need five men. All she needed was *a* God-fearing man, and, as my Bishop taught me in one of his books; entitled: *"all you need, is a good brain washing"*. And all her hurt and pain from worldly letdowns would've went away. If he's really committed to a life with his God, then he'll has a God to answer to: someone who holds him accountable. That's why I wrote that you need a **God-fearing man,** not just a **church-goer:** because the more you give of yourself, the more you lose of you, and you're not equally yoked if your man is not God-fearing and you are. The devil goes to church," but he is not God-fearing. Actually, your spouse should add to you in every way — *physically, mentally, spiritually, domestically, and financially.* Because I am equally yoked with my wife, I'm better today because of her and vice-versa.

Some women today are just settling for a man with a *"ding-a-ling;"* no God or kickstand. I know you know what I mean when I say no God; so, let's talk about that kickstand. When you finish riding your bike, you park it and put the kickstand down to keep your bike from falling over and hitting the ground. Well, that's a quality woman should look for in a man: someone with a *good kick stand* to keep you both from falling.

True story: A friend of mine who was a heavy drinker became very ill because of her alcohol abuse and had to be admitted to the hospital. Her family and friends all came to the hospital, crying, hoping, and praying for her to get well. While in the waiting room, the family started to talk about how she got in such a bad condition. They wondered how she had fallen so far so fast that she was now so sick. Soon enough, they learned that she was suffering from alcohol poisoning. Her body just broke down from drinking too much. Most of the family members in the waiting room started pointing the finger at the man she lived with, the boyfriend. Trust me on this one: stay away from *live-in boyfriends and playboys.* You ask why? I'm glad you asked. A live-in boyfriend is playing house and a playboy is just playing.

The sister of the sick woman said to the boyfriend, *"She's like this because of YOU!"* He replied, "She's grown, and she can drink all she wants, when she wants." Maybe that's why the word of God says, "be ye not unequally yoked together with unbelievers." Obviously, there are two gods in one house: A God of righteousness and a god of unrighteousness; light and darkness; good and bad; you name it, it was in there. This woman's boyfriend was a man with no kickstand. He said, "She can drink all she wants when she wants." A man with a kickstand would've said to the woman, "honey that's enough," and he would've helped her get on the road to sobriety or to a social drinker, never a drunk. There is no way a man who loves God and says he loves you is going to let you fall or let you abuse yourself. Still today women yoke up with men whose actions speak as loudly as Adam when he said to God, *"the woman you gave me, said eat the apple."* That man has no kickstand! It's clear to see that this man has no compass or "kickstand," so why are you with him? Oh, he has a ding-a-ling, but that ding-a-ling and the penalties for not being a lady first are going to cause you to miss the things that God has for you and maybe cause you to lose your life. If your live-in can't keep you from falling, you don't need him. There is truth in the saying, *"I can do bad all by myself."* Because if he really wants you, he will make the investment in you and put a ring on your finger. Come on ladies and step up your game!

I'll never forget when my wife and I started to date, and I decided to have some wine with my dinner. She stopped me right in my tracks and said, *"Aren't you saved?"* I said, Yes. Remember, we were dating, not married. This is a teachable moment because if your partner is going along with your sin, maybe you need to date a little longer as believers before marriage. Marriage is a lifetime commitment and you don't want a man or woman who will let, or help you fall. Wine is not a sin, but it's the little fox that destroys the vine. In other words, she stopped me from falling before I even stumbled, that's what Godly people do for one another: like kickstands on bikes, they help you to stand. When this boyfriend said, *"She drinks when she wants, as much as she wants,"* that should have been the first and last sign for that woman that she was unequally yoked. **(This is a sidebar)... I wanted to clock him. (like ring his bell) No, smile. No, lol).** My friend should not have walked out of his life; she should have run fast, because people like that will set you up for death by offering you sin.

Today you need somebody who will offer you life, not death. Please remember this for the rest of your life. When he says, "I love you," remember it only takes a minute to fall in love, *but a lifetime to build.* So, if he's not building with you, what's the point? Remember this also regarding relationships so you will know when things are going South, not on vacation with you but solo.

Great story; Remember when you first met, fell in love, and were dating and while you were at the club with him, the photographer and the flower guy would say, *"Would you like to buy the pretty lady some flowers?"* Six months or less into the relationship, he would say, "Give her a dozen!" Six months to a year into the relationship, when the flower guy asked about roses, he would say to you, Honey, do you want *A* rose? He went from a dozen to one rose less than a year. Then, a year later, you go to the same club and the flower guy says, "Would you like to buy the pretty lady a rose," ...and he yells, beating his chest as he says, "She don't need no rose, *I'm her rose!"* Trust me, the relationship you thought you had, has now just jumped onto 95 South at 100 mph, with no passengers: it has gotten away from you. Keep this thought in your memory rolodex you'll need it one day.

Back to the woman at the well.... I didn't know the woman at the well or what she was looking for; but she was not looking for another ding-a-ling. You must remember that the more you give of yourself, the more you lose of you. Ladies get this scripture deep in your spirit, because even if you have a bad marriage or relationship, for whatever reason, if the both of you are yoked up with God, He's able to keep you from falling. Please! (put a praise right there) ...

Jude 1: 24 (ESV)
Now to him who can keep you
from stumbling, (falling).

Paul addressed the Corinthians to stay away from developing dangerous affections with other gods, and who you yoke up with. Not all unbelievers are sinners; some just haven't accepted Christ yet. But sin all by itself is deadly, and wicked, and destructive. Make no mistake about it, sin is deadlier than stage 4 terminal cancer, Aids, Ebola, the Zika virus, and jumping out of an airplane at 30,000 feet without a parachute, all at the same time. That's how deadly sin is. *I hope that helped.* The devil came for one reason, and it's documented in the word of God:

John 10:10 (ESV)
The thief comes only to steal
and kill and destroy.

To reiterate; Jude 1:24 reminds us that when we put our trust in God, *"he will keep us from falling or stumbling."* Man will let you fall and that's bad; but an unsaved man will let you split your head open to the *white meat.* Jude used the word stumble to indicate that the person is moving, because a person not walking or running can't fall or stumble unless he or she faints. The moving person can stumble. Women, you're on the move. Don't stop or slow down for a *ding-a-ling, broken compass or kickstand* who will let you fall. God is saying

He's able to keep you from stumbling or falling if you don't give yourself a way to unequal yoked situation. God has made you for one man and if you trust God, that man will be a God-fearing man. The penalties for not being a lady first are bad enough; the last thing you need is a man who doesn't have a God conscience.

God is so invested in your success that He said He will present you faultless. The Samaritan woman had relationships with six men. God is saying his investment in you means more to him than six husbands. I'm not saying God is happy with her sin. I'm saying God is bigger than her sin. He says He's going to present us faultless. When you are faultless, you have no blemish. God is showing the Samaritan woman He's going to present her -- and us other sinners -- as faultless. I believe this woman got herself so deep into sin that she couldn't find a way out; and because Jesus is indeed a rock in a weary land, when she hit rock bottom, He sensed her distress and had to go see about her in Samaria. If I could say one thing to this woman, and to women in general, it would be it's never too late for **true love**; just make sure it's connected to Jesus.

Most women today have been lied to for so long, that most, though not all of them could call men Scooby-Doo -- you know: dogs. That's not true. Men are not dogs; they're like anyone else who does not have a God conscience. They're loose. When a woman calls a man a dog yet she's screwing him, what does that say about her? When women have kids by a man who moves on or she has children by different fathers, that clock starts ticking. You should not make permanent decisions on temporary situations like the **old biological clock.** That's the wrong way to look for love. Just stick to the plan...God's plan.

Jeremiah 29:11 (ESV)
For I know the plans I have for you, declares
the Lord, plans for welfare and not for evil, to
give you a future and a hope.

God said the thoughts He has for you are thoughts of peace. So, if you have strange men coming into and out of your life you are not living a life of peace. Earlier, I said God will keep you from stumbling or falling. In other words, don't grow weary in your well doing. You are moving and doing well. Don't be a jump off – a source of temporary relief – for a man. Don't let just any man have his way with you. Enjoy living holy and embrace your salvation, especially while you're single, living a life of liberty and joy. This is the best time of your life! When was the last time someone said that to you, *precious lady?* I have nothing against marriage, but when you're single you have time to choose who and what you think you want. My wife doesn't like it when I say this, but everybody should get married; if their dating, so they can see what it's really like, **why should they have all the fun seeing who they want, when they want.** She thinks it's a put down of marriage, but I'm saying that marriage is actually a wonderful thing when it is built on God's solid foundation. But at the same time lots of work.

Galatians 6:9 (ESV)
And let us not grow weary of doing good,
for in due season we will reap,
if we do not give up.

One of the biggest penalties for not being a lady first is when you let the flesh control you. Remember this saying: *"the flesh will send you to hell and won't show up."* The more you give of yourself, the more you lose of you. Every day, men and women are losing when their flesh takes the lead.

I'm convinced that if mankind will go back to the old landmark, the Bible, we all would be better off. Sin is killing the human race. Jesus made it to the Samaritan woman in time, but will he get to you in time? Our government is breaking all of God's laws and replacing them with straight sin... No chaser. If you were ever a drinker, you know that if you don't put soda, juice, or ice in your drink, you're going to get drunk fast, and you could lose your life. So, we must get back to God before it's too late. One of the biggest mistake's mankind made concerning the word of God is not just hearing from God, which is a huge mistake, but it's not the worst. The worst mistake would be hearing from God, and not doing what you hear.

One of the tragic stories is the tale of Samson and Delilah, even though Sampson knew God's spirit and voice, he couldn't get out of his own way. To say the woman Delilah brought him down would be misleading and would not lay the blame correctly, to the devil's attack on mankind. The thing that brings most people down is not having their flesh in check. Delilah was the least of Sampson's problems. Sampson's trouble came when his flesh was his leader. If you look at the history of mankind, when it hit its lowest points, you'll see that not just sin was involved, but the flesh. *"Stinking Thinking"* was at the helm. We can't point the finger at Eve or "woman" alone. Man, was, and is, just as much of the problem. If you look at the Bible the way God gave it to us in the beginning,

He gave man and woman dominion over the earth. So, really man is the one messing thing's up by trying to run everything. The woman is just going along for the ride, and it's time to stop that process. The penalties for not being a lady first cause woman to lose their self-respect; while men are heroes. The only problem with that is our young men will follow the same (chauvinism) path and it must stop!

Women should know that the more they give of themselves, the more they lose of themselves. Little boys are growing up without fathers and bringing all the hurt and pain with them into adulthood relationships; and that's another penalty for not being a lady first. We have to get back to Jesus fully dressed, not only by clothing our bodies, but our minds, as well.

We all should do a better job of controlling our flesh, especially women because of the way the world think of them. When a woman leaves a man, most of the time the man moves on with his life. But when a man tries to leave a woman with a child, whether that child is here or on the way, it's a lifetime soap opera; a real **(Days of Our Lives, As the world turns)** or he'll just live one day and die if she had her way... Everybody gets hurt. The woman's heart is broken, the child feels abandoned, and in the woman's head, the man must be dealt with, we all know what that means.

Another penalty for not being a lady first is ending up living a bittersweet – or sweet to bitter – life. We must get back to Jesus, and we must stop giving men permission to leave. We all did it, (abandon our woman and family's) but that doesn't make it right. A fighter is trained to stick and move to protect himself from his opponent, **but a**

father is to stick and stay with his partner. Who gave men permission to leave anyway? Their fathers. And who gave their fathers permission to leave? Their fathers' fathers... See, we all lose when we forget God's laws, so now the penalties are not just on the women, but on mankind. We must get back to God because, as you see, the more you give of yourself, the more you lose of you. That goes both ways, so now this Samaritan woman is trying to get back to her first love, (Jesus). Isn't that what most people are looking for, love in some of the wrong places? that doesn't make you bad, it makes you not focus on long term goals for you and yours.

This woman said to Jesus, sir, give me this water that I may not thirst nor have to come here to draw again. Often, it seems, when a woman gets with a man, she's not looking for another man. In most cases, the woman starts out as a faithful partner. When a man lets a woman down, he doesn't know it at the time, but he just wrecked her world. On the other hand, when a woman lets a man down, he is likely just to move on to the next thing, with no harm intended, in some cases. Men have been letting women down for so long, that now women do the same things men do. Women move on now, when really all along the woman setting up shop in her head. She's making plans for home with this man in her head. When the man is finished doing the **nasty** with the woman, he moves on; but the woman is shopping for curtains, drapes, and carpet for her home with this man that she just did the nasty with.

This behavior must stop. Because too many people are getting hurt behind sex disguised as love. When the following revelation was downloaded into my spirit, I didn't want to hear it, my Spirit man was happy, but my flesh said… *"What the!!! **We don't have the right to have sex unmarried.**You* may not want to face that fact, but it's the truth. If we broke man's laws the way we break God's law, some of us would be doing life without parole. Now you know God had to drop that in my Spirit, because I would have been the first in a *State or County jumpsuit doing life…* but thanks be to God who gives us the victory through our Lord Jesus Christ.

1 Corinthians 15:57 (ESV)
But thanks be to God, who gives us the victory
through our Lord Jesus Christ.

Because of God's victory through Jesus, we have been able to overcome sin, and we will continue to overcome. Victory comes from God. Let's stop wasting time fooling ourselves. Without God, we are nothing. We are giving ourselves away to the wrong people. This Samaritan woman is just trying to get back home, like some of us. She asked Jesus to give her drink, so she wouldn't have to come back to this self-serving situation anymore and lose her soul. Jesus mentioned the woman's husband in order to expose her sin, not to harm her, but to free her from six losers, and the woman admitted, *"I have No husband."*

John 4:16 (ESV)
Jesus said to her, "Go, call your husband,
and come here."

I don't want to make this a long story, but I know guys who will commit just enough crimes to get off the streets for those three to four months during the winter season. They are just tired of life and in need of a break. No doubt, this woman was tired of being let down by men, and she just wanted to get away. When Jesus came, she said give me... just give me because anything is better than these Five Guys + 1... and I'm not talking about the burger guys. She just was tired, and Jesus basically said to her, *"Come unto me, and I will give you rest."*

My brothers and sisters let us all get back to Jesus before it's too late.

Just surrender all like the woman at the well. I don't want to leave you hanging about my statement that you don't have the right to have sex unmarried, so, let's say it another way: you don't have the right to have sex un-blessed.

Genesis 1:28 (ESV)
And God blessed them. And God said to
them, "Be fruitful and multiply and fill the
earth and subdue it,

In this scripture, God gave Adam and Eve permission to have sex and have children. Then He blessed them. Do you see all the Them's? Most of our problems come from disobedience, because God never gave you and me permission to have sex outside of his blessing, but He gave them permission through His blessing of their union. When this Samaritan woman found out she was outside of God's will, she literally said, *take these little boys,* I'm having sex with and give me you, and every blessing that comes with you. When she said give me drink, she was actually saying, *"I surrender all to you."* She didn't want to fight or plead her case; she just wanted out. I believe women today just want out — of the ups and downs of being the *"help meet"* who is getting no help. All most women want is you, a man that can keep his promises. When she gave herself to you, all she wanted was you in return; all of you. I for one don't think that's asking too much, you? It's a beautiful thing when the relationship is blessed by God.

Remember, the more you give of yourself the more you lose of you. So, stop giving yourself away to just anybody; if you have never had true love, you don't know what you're missing. God gives it just like He gives life; and let me tell you, it's a beautiful thing...

One more quick story.... My wife might go off on me for telling you this, but I'll take one for the team! We were going through some hard times in our marriage and we started to pray about the situation. While praying, we started to worship and weep. After that, we cuddled and cried together. Before you knew it, **(close your ears in-laws and young ins) lol...** we were making love: anointed, old fashioned, hot, steamy, moist sex... Oh my mouth just got wet.... I'm sorry; I went too far. --but remember, I'm taking one for the team... and I'm talking about my helpmate. The point I'm making is that when you are in a union that is blessed, and you are equally yoked with your partner, it's like that all the time. Now, if you want to learn more about *"you don't have the right to have sex,"* keep reading. It's in full details in one of the chapters in the book. And remember, the more you give of yourself, the more you lose of you.

Chapter 3

I Have Seen It All

2 Corinthians 4:18 (ESV)
*as we look not to the things that are seen but
to the things that are unseen. For the things
that are seen are transient, but the things that
are unseen are eternal.*

Oh, have I seen it all. My goal for writing this book is to give you the knowledge to take you from earth to Glory fully dress in every way. This is a very touchy chapter because you can't tell people how to dress or how to present themselves, but for the book sake, you must understand that your dress code is everything to your success in this life, especially if you're looking for a husband, a good relationship, job or just want to live a full, classy life. *And remember the things that are unseen are eternal.*

Most women don't have a clue about how a man feels about another man seeing his goods, or the way you present yourself, especially in public, which means everything to the man in your life. That's the way we do appraisals before we invest in you. *(Hang on to that info for life! Trust me You'll need it.)* The man himself wants to see everything you've got, but for his eyes only. Have you ever wondered why when he met you in the streets or in the club, your outfit didn't seem to matter to him? But once he committed to you, he wanted you to wear a full-length miniskirt dragging the floor, why, because he knows what attracted him to you and he does not want any more bee's to find his honey. It is very important to be mindful of what you wear and show, because most men have *seen it all...* Oh yeah, from tube tops, thongs leg-in-and-outs, all the way down to mini-everything. Why do you think Victoria called it a secret? It's for you and your one man or husband, not for everybody on the street to see. That's where the beach whistle came from, the real name is the *(wolf whistle)* girls showing everything in a swimsuit. That was then, before you were in a committed relationship; this is now, so let's work on getting it right.

I'll never forget when I was in the world and I introduced a friend of mine to a young lady. One day we were at the house just lounging around. She was there also and had a surprise for him, me too, we just didn't know it. She went in the back room and from out of nowhere she came out of the bedroom in a teddy showing both *buttock cheeks.* In other words, she put on a real show for both of us. He had just met her about two or three months earlier. She didn't know, but my buddy had committed to her, and in his mind, what she had was for his eyes only. As she walked by us showing her new teddy, *(Victoria secret)* dude, my friend jumped off the couch like a sprinter doing a 100-yard dash; like a cheetah on a gazelle and covered her up with his body, *talk about the bodyguard!* like she belonged to him. Well, she did, because he had seen it all with her before. Now she was not wifey; she was property, because he'd seen it all. Once that happens, one lady is a married woman someone loves and respects; the other lady is someone who is owned by a person like a slave, to be used as needed. Please be careful about advertising all your goods because some men don't know where to draw the line. Some men will just do everything that husbands are authorized to do because they were never given boundaries. You have to guard yourself like a fence or an imaginary line that shows where one area ends, and another area begins, or a point or limit that indicates where two things become different.

Once a man who is not your husband sees your private parts, he knows he has no official rules. In that situation, a man will just go in with no limits that define acceptable behavior. There used to be a time when you could have said if I can touch it I can get it. Now it's like what <u>Flip Wilson </u>said in his Geraldine comedy routine: ***"What you see is what you get, Sucker!"*** Please stop showing all your goods. What I'm giving you is classic 101, page 5 in the player's hand book.

Still today I haven't gotten over my friend jumping off the couch stopping the peep show of the woman, I introduced to him. He was selfish; just thinking about himself. Remember I said I was in the world. Most men know that if she is showing it, she wants someone to get it. Maybe not now but someday I don't make the ways of the world; I just see those ways, just like you. If you're ever going to get the respect you deserve you must stop putting yourself on display before strangers. By all means, dress yourself to show that you are pretty; but you should leave something to the imagination. A man should use his mind and draw a picture in his head. The picture should not be walking by him in *living color.* That show is for home, between husband and wife boyfriend, girlfriend he and he or she and she whatever just keep it private. If he sees it, who else has seen it? He doesn't necessarily want you; he wants what he sees... your butt.

I was at the gym one day and some women walked in as some guys were lifting weights. Suddenly everyone stopped working out as the women walked in the gym wearing shorts that showed everything... *creases, hammer toe, camel foot and pig's feet;* you name it. It was open season for free feet's Lol... Just like that we made our moves on those women. Our goal was not to love and respect them but to screw them, because they aroused our loins. Those women left no room for the imagination, just the lower parts moved. That's what is happening every day to women who have this kind of dress code; and men go in like sharks with no remorse for their actions because there were not thinking with the head above their shoulders. They were not thinking at all. The dress code was the invitation with no boundaries, and the guidelines or limits were what those women let us see... all their goods. Those women used their attire to send a message to us: *I'm showing you all of what you're missing, and you can have.* Look, I want you to see who is showing off all the stuff that doesn't belong to him, so you know who's really behind all evil.

Luke 4:5 (ESV)
And the devil took him up and showed him all the kingdoms of the world in a moment of time,

Using the following scripture, I want to show you with verifiable facts that what the devil is showing you doesn't even belong to him:

Psalm 115:16 (ESV)
The heavens are the Lord's heavens,
but the earth he has given to the
children of man.

Not only is the devil showing off stuff that's not his, he's showing off our stuff. He's showing Jesus, stuff that God gave to us. *Ladies put a lid on it.* And put your clothes back on. Have you ever watched an artist start drawing a picture and at first you don't know what it's going to look like, but the more the artist works on the canvas, the more you can see what the picture is? Well, the same goes for dressing: the way you present yourself paints the picture of who you are. It's almost like telling a story about yourself. When a lady of the evening goes out to work, she dressed in a way to tell her customers – her Johns -- that she's open for business. She doesn't say it; she shows it. The same goes for *Wall Street or Wal-Mart.* People dress for the service they're giving. When you see the postman in uniform you're looking for mail, not a hamburger. The same goes with your uniform or dress code. Have you ever heard the saying *"dress for success"?* When people dress in a provocative way in public, they are showing some signs of insecurity. Showing your spouse all your goods is a great thing but showing all of yourself to strangers is another story. When you dress provocatively in public, your man sees you and all of his friends see you also. They see inside and out; upside and down the other, not a good look for your success in that relationship. You always need to make a good first impression. Can you imagine where a young man's mind goes when he sees your butt crack? Think about it. Every organ in his body wakes up, looking to penetrate your body; not to love and respect you, but to release passion or emotions that come and go. A feeling like that has the power to hurt or kill everything in its path. Even though your butt looks good I might add, you have managed to attract Mr. Wrong. Always remember this: *you only get one chance to make a first impression.*

Today, so many people have decided if the manufacturer makes it, I'm going to wear it. **Not so.** Just because someone makes it doesn't mean everyone is supposed to wear it. When someone is a size 5, certain clothing are made for her; however, someone who is a size 25 wide plus plus, cannot wear the same outfit. Well she could but not a good look! There used to be a time when the older women would teach the younger women how to secure their places as future brides. Today it seems like some older women are acting like younger women. It's true that times have changed, but men making future investments in loose women is still the same: one-night stands, never wifey. Ouch… Save something for the future honeymoon. I know everybody does not want to be a wife, or so I have heard, so dress in a way that shows you have respect for yourself. If a man won't cover you, cover yourself. One of the things I don't think women understand is the way you carry yourself is setting the foundation for the women who come after you. Your daughters will dress and act just like you in some regards. You're a role model for them. In some cases, the way you carry yourself is the way your daughter will carry herself. If you're a lady, she will model you, but if you're a tramp, nine times out of ten she will follow you too.

A friend told me a story about a young woman who came to church wearing shorts up to her neck and a see-through everything. My friend said she was shocked but kept an open mind about the way the woman was dressed: thinking maybe that's all she has, and we should thank God she's here. My friend decided to embrace the philosophy of letting them come in first, then we'll teach them the right way. In other, less elegant words, *catch the fish first, then clean it.* Then another thought entered my friend's mind: *would she go to work in that attire?* Perhaps the young woman thought she was pleasing her man or that she could catch a man dressed that way; or maybe she just didn't know church etiquette. Either way, her value was dropping, and dropping fast. Ladies never devalue yourself for anyone, because you only get one time to make a first impression. If you're going to show something, show your value and your intelligence, not your private parts. Somebody is going to love you for showing him one day. But remember that when you show all your goods publicly, people label you as easy, loose, wild, or provocative. Jesus came that you might have life, I'm writing so you will have the advantage and win in the relationship game of life.

Here is a priceless message for all the garment-deprived people. There is nothing that a man likes better than a well-dressed lady. The way she carries herself; the way her dress, blouse, or pants cling to her body when she walks -- not tightly but showcasing the unseen the right way: ever so lightly. It makes him think of what could be. He's undressing you with his thoughts, not eyes. The phrase *the chase is better than the catch* is very appropriate here. Leave something for the imagination in the relationship game. You can document that and work it at your discretion.

That's the secret -- the magic -- to getting him to take care of you and keep his promises. Help him use his imagination, because most men have seen it all. Most men think while dating, *if I've seen it, he's seen it.* So, the less you show, the better off you are in the short and long runs. Trust me, his imagination about you will keep the fire burning way after midnight. That may not sound like much but, *Baby Doll*... I just save you a lifetime of heart hack, let downs and disappoints with your (Boo)...

Have you ever wondered why some men have girlfriends forever, in strictly platonic *(heterosexual)* relationships? It's the imagination gone wild. The fun about the imagination is, it's endless. What he can't get right now, he imagines. *(Something like the million-dollar lottery)*, we dream about all of what where going to do with the money if we win, and how were going to tell our boss's where to go!... Smile. I'm going to stop talking about that imagination thing before I get in trouble. Ladies know that I just gave you chapter #1 out of the player's handbook. Use it at your discretion, *sorry fella's.* We owed her that...Now, where was I?... Oh, here we go...

As a man, I was taught to dress to impress, not to attract. When you dress to attract, it's like catching fish with a net. You don't know what you're going to get because the killer is out there, as well. So, always strive to impress, never to attract, it's better than hearing the *(wolf whistle)* when you walk by. That's the low end. Most guys have seen it all, so if you want to give a man something he never had, present yourself as a **(lady with proprietary rights).** I know that sometimes it seems that when you get all dressed up looking good, everyone will say something nice to you except the person you want to say something nice.

Ladies watch what you show and who you show it to. You don't want to be prey for other people's weakness or brokenness. In other words, the devil is always seeking. If you only knew the people who hooked up with bums because of the way, they were dressed.

You showed too much flesh and attracted *"Snoop Doggie Bow Wow;" or MR. Kelly first name R* that sees only one thing good in you: your butt. That was one of your greatest assets and you showed the killer your *money maker* right out of the gate. He liked it and followed you home and now you can't get rid of him. You told him to stop calling you, but that's not what you showed him. In the world, seeing is believing If you have ever watched the gambling channel, you know that the players never show their aces and they never ever show facial expressions. They keep straight faces so the other guys at the table don't know what's in their hands or head. That's how you win in the game: holding your best cards close to you, to show only when the other players put their cards on the table. Then and only then can you show your cards, so you're not played. Maybe you need to take a page out of the gamblers' handbook and stop showing you're *(a-s-s-e-t-s)* to everybody at the table. You have to believe in your aces (talent, beauty) the gifts God gave you, so you can win in the game of life and stop being a victim to people with low self-esteem.

Most of the time when you're dressed in a provocative way, you're going to attract the lower nature of some men -- and, sad to say, women also -- looking for lust at your peep show. That could be a major problem for some people because some guys don't know what no means or even understand no because he probably can't read; especially Slick Rick. That's what people call a person that live a trickery life. When we were kids in grammar school, we had a thing called show and tell where we would bring a toy or object of some kind to class and have time to show the other kids and tell them something about the toy or thing they might not knew. The problem with dressing loosely as a lady is that you're showing and telling at the same time another story without opening your mouth. Some guys read you the wrong way before you tell them what the deal is and off he goes.

A lady friend was telling me a story about a lady she met while out with some mutual friends. One of the ladies had on pumps and a mini-skirt. Well at first, everyone thought she was very loose because she was dressed that way at a formal event. When she opened her mouth, my friend said, she spoke well and was very classy and intelligent. My friend went on to say, *"when the lady opened her mouth, the voice didn't go with her dress code."* Her eloquent speech floored people, but her dress code took center stage and robbed her of her credibility. She brought attention to her body and not to her brain. Like many women, she put her power in the wrong place. Remember: you only get one time to make a first impression.

For instance, when we go to a restaurant or a store, we get to see what's on the menu or on the racks to buy. That's how most stores or restaurants sell their products. Well, when you dress and show all your stuff, you're putting your products on the menu for sale, also. Ladies, when you show all your goods to a man, you show him what's on the menu for sale, and after he sees it, he wants to buy with cash for time. Watch what you put on the menu for the public to see. Notice of a foreclosure is public information. You're not.

Let's look at the metaphor that some women use: *"men are dogs."* People use that term to refer to lose men who sleep around with multiple women. Metaphorically speaking, then, if a man is a dog, then a woman would be the bone. You know what dogs do with bones: they chew and lick them for a while, then they bury them. One day, the dog will dig that bone up to chew, lick, and bury again; in other words, to use for his pleasure. But what you see as just a bone is full of nutrition. Have you ever wondered why dogs bury their bones? its so other dogs don't find their bone and take it for themselves. The bone is the hard piece of the body called the skeleton the part that holds the body together. The dog knows instinctively that most of the vitamins and nutrition are in the marrow of the bone, that why he buries to use again one day.

That's what most men know about women: they have hidden value. It's time that the ladies know also that they have great stuff on the inside. Ladies what you're giving as a bone has more nutrition than the meat on the inside. Stop giving your bones as junk and stop showing off all your meats. You're not a meat locker; you're a lady: ***God's highest expression in the earth with great value inside of you.*** Every part of you has great value, the meat, bone and the skin. Most men know that if they're going to make it, they're going to need their bones, so they don't fall apart so, they bury them, and it has to stop! He overcompensates when he sees too much meat because he's seen it all and he knows the value of what you're giving away. He is finding, licking, chewing, and burying it for another day. Ladies stop giving your bones away for free. Most men know and see your value; they just don't know where to place that value. Most of us men don't know what a diamond in the rough looks like.

The problem is greed. It's hard for a man with Christ leading and guiding him to stay with one woman. Do you know how hard it is for a heathen, pimp, sugar daddy, or regular Joe to just stay with one bone? It's almost impossible without Christ. (Don't ask me why). He has no one to keep him together; and you know we are not the best housekeepers, so we go as long as we can just getting bones and burying them, trying to stay together! Using people when it's convenient for you is lazy and selfish. That's why you must watch what you show and tell.

The word of God tells us that when Jesus died, he left the Holy Spirit to lead and guide us into all truth. If your man is not being led by the Holy Spirit, what's leading him? You may say it is his head leading him.... But which one?

John 16:13 (ESV)
When the Spirit of truth comes, he will
guide you into all the truth,

This is Jesus speaking to the apostles in this scripture about His impending death. He is assuring them that He is leaving the Holy Spirit to help them as they live their everyday lives and to reveal all about His life and death. Now, if the apostles needed guidance to understand the truth, what makes you think that a mortal guy you call a dog doesn't need help? When a man sees your breast, he doesn't care about anything else for that moment. So, ladies: *less brawn and more brains.*

If you get nothing else out of this book, ladies get this: men -- not just your man or some men – but all men are Visual. In other words, when he sees, he understands, and can relate. When it's appealing, it's easy for him to understand, not love and respect, but understand. When you tell him something, he doesn't know what you're talking about, but when you show him, it all makes sense to him. What you show him appeals to his senses, one of the five natural powers we all possess: *touch, taste, sight, smell, and hearing.* That is what we all need for information to navigate in this life, but none of the five senses touch the heart.

Ladies, you touched him, but in the wrong five places, all of which are physical. It's a feeling, something that our bodies experience, and that's just an emotion. Tina Turner called love a *second-hand emotion.* We all know emotions -- *love, anger, joy, hate and fear* -- come and go. Ladies, you don't want your man to <u>emotion</u> you. You want him to <u>cover</u> you with love like Christ covered and loved the church and gave his life for it.

I hope you don't think that is asking too much of your man, because marriages and relationships should continue until death do you part. If that's asking too much, maybe he's the wrong one!

We take relationships too lightly. In my study and research, I found out something about homelessness and relationships are distant cousins. Some people may think when someone is homeless it's an economic or money thing. Well, that's not the whole truth; most people are homeless because of relationships, or more accurately, a breakdown in relationships. Case in point: when a family or marriage breaks up, people lose touch. If the person in the breakup falls on hard times, if the relationship is not still intact, the person has nowhere to go if that's his or her only family in the area, so they end up on the street, shelters etc.... If the relationship was still strong, you could sleep in the quest room or on the floor or on the couch until you get on your feet. That's how strong relationships should be, and marriages should be even stronger than that! Relationships and homelessness have a lot in common, so if you can't keep the marriage, keep the relationship. It may keep you off the street.

Let's look at the fig tree in the word of God, and maybe we'll see why having on your garments is so important to God and your future.

Matthew 21:19 (ESV)
And seeing a fig tree by the wayside, he went
to it and found nothing on it but only leaves.
And he said to it, "May no fruit ever come from
you again!" And the fig tree withered at once.

Jesus is teaching a parable *(a short story)* that provides a moral or spiritual lesson. Jesus was hungry and desired to eat of the fruit of the fig tree one more time before his death. He could not because fig trees do not bear their fruit in the spring, but in the fall of the year; however, fig trees do have a small edible fruit that appears in the spring before the sprouting of the leaves. This tree was full of leaves but was empty of fruit. It was looking full of promises, but empty, like some of us.

Ladies, when you dress in a way that shows everything to a man, just like Jesus saw the fig tree, you are saying **come and enjoy my fruits.** To the man, you're saying, when you are half dressed, don't read the whole book, let the cover of my leaves tell my story; just come and eat. The leaves on the tree were a sign that you can come and eat fruit. Ladies, being half dressed has a sign of its own to men. It's like a bad storm, a mixed bag of tricks like a nor'easter... (Wind that rotates counterclockwise) you're going to get a little bit of everything, but no fruit. We don't like to be fooled. We want to get what we want or paid for. This is what most people look like when they're half-dressed: *looking full of promises, but empty.* The truth is, your leaves, or the lack of them, are exposing you.... The fruit in your life is the *secret sauce* that everybody wants. Meat or bone, most men want it; so, cover yourself, not just with leaves, but fruit. When the fall comes, the leaves fall away, and your fruit will be exposed with no protection, but if you walk in integrity when your season comes, and it will, the R-E-S-P-E-C-T will remain. If the players club boss knew what I was about to tell you. I would lose my players card, smile... Pay Attention.

When a man says to a woman, *"give me more time when it comes to relationships,"* what he is really saying in short *is* give me more time to screw you to see if this is what I really want; or give me more time to have fun with you until wifey comes along. It's a cold world out there. Either way, you lose; so, know your talent, value and worth, and put your clothes back on because if he finds you without fruit or clothing on, just like Jesus cursed the fig tree for having empty promises; so, will your boo.

So many times, the woman is left to fend for herself for one reason or another and the fruit ends up going bad, mainly because the woman gives or shows the man something he wasn't ready for. Who's to blame? Most of the time, the man because he will beg her until she can't say no anymore. Either way, the fruit goes bad for two reasons. Ladies, once a man has his way with you, your value goes way down. (When the guys find out what I'm revealing to you, I might be on the run, so leave the porch light on....) So, now you once could've been wifey but now you're just his boo. You are number two, which is natural and physical --*poop*. The next thing you know, you are a woman with a new name: *sour*, because you thought you would be his choice when you gave him what he begged you for. Most men can beg harder than Keith, Teddy, Kelly, Freddy, and Luther all at the same time and lie like carpet on the floor, so watch who you let eat your fruit. Oh my, did I say that?

Ladies, the key to getting, having, and keeping a man is never to lose your advantage. Let's keep it real, your advantage is your vagina, *(really, it's your brains)* but who using brains today surely not cougars, because men don't beg you for food or garments, we... I mean he ...begs you for your stuff. Girls I'm on the run now, let's keep our relationship. *You got somewhere I can stay?*

Jesus cursed the fig tree because He desired to eat from it, ladies, men have one desire from woman and God made it that way, and that's to have relationship with you, that's the bottom line Until you build a relationship it is what it is. *(Yes, we want all of you)* ... but that's after we build a relationship with you. I'm married 20 years now and I be looking at my wife all the time trying to have relations with her, that's why I say you got to build a relationship first, because it only takes a minute to fall in love, but a lifetime to build, now you have to know it and use it to your advantage; not for selfish gain, but to build your family and life. Your desire is to your husband, not just any old Joe. Remember, you are bone of Adam's bone and if you're going to be successful in this life as a leading lady, you must know where your strengths are; and I'm not talking between your legs; I'm talking about the strength you have to make a man keep his promise. There's a formula to make a man take care of you and everything connected to you, and it's not just your beauty or your booty. It's your gifting and your timing to know when. You have great gifts to bring to the table. Kenny Rogers said it best, in one of his Hit songs, *"You got to know when to hold them."* When you look at most successful women, one of the qualities you will find is that she knows who and whose she is. Like some of the great women in the bible and in our world today, before she held her man in bed she held him in his business affairs. Believe it or not, most men are looking for love also, but in the wrong places. You must help them along the way and let him know not just who you are, but who he is as a *(Kings Kid)* ... If you just let him have his way with you, then you're a part of the problem; meeting his wants, but never his needs.

I was sharing with a friend one day about my deliverance from the world systems. I said to him, I'm so glad God didn't give me what I deserved, but He gave me what I needed. That's one of the reasons why men go through so many women, because so many women meet his wants and his needs are starving suffering from malnutrition. When you show him all your goods, he goes for it with no regard for who he hurts. Ladies, the responsibility is back on you. When he comes with his manhood hanging out, swinging all over the place, it's your job to cut it off (Ouch) -- not detach it from his body, but from going into your body. Until you see your body as a highly valued, important, and sacred place that deserves great respect, you can forget about a man giving you the respect that you deserve. Oh, yeah, you'll get it, sex but you won't get him.

As I was growing up trying to understand dating and relationships, I found myself with women I really didn't want to be with, but I stayed for the ride, (you know sex). One of the things my mother said to me I'll never forget. After finding out I was involved with women on a superficial level, just going through the motions, she said to me, *"Tony if you don't mean the girl no good, leave her alone."* That's still my motto today.

I once went out with a woman who thought she could walk in and out of my life. Well, one day she did. She broke up with me just to get back together again. *(You know: "make up to break up; that's all we do. First you love me, then you hate me).* And I went for it until she did it again and tried to come back. Well, she found out that mama taught me right and I thought I was in love If I let her come back a second time, she would have lost all respect for me and dogged me out, but remember I thought I was in love. She came back, but my heart wasn't in it, and all I did was use her. Then I remembered what mama said: if you're not going to do her right, let her go. So, I did, and thank goodness I did. If I had let her walk in and out of my life, she would have walked all over me.

Ladies, he may walk in and he may walk out, but don't you let anybody walk in and out of your life because he will never ever respect you. You will be the bone licked and buried all your life, because men have seen it all. If you want to show a man something new, show him the lady you are. Just like you, most men are tired of empty promises, so the next time he shakes your tree -- and believe me, he will -- be full of promises, not bones to bury. The problem with the leaves not being on the tree when Jesus was hungry was the season. If leaves are on the tree, fruit should be there also. In other words, there's a season for everything. Please wait on your season. Ladies you can't continue to show your fruit out of season without it going bad, because you are allowing it to be harvested in the wrong season. So, cover up and protect your fruit. When he comes to you, and he will, your fruit will remain un-touched, un-picked, and un-plucked until the right season—(man) -- comes into your life. It's time out for looking full of promises, but being empty, because most men have seen it all.

Chapter 4

The Power of One Woman

2 Samuel 11:2 (ESV)
David arose from his couch and was walking
on the roof of the king's house, that he saw
from the roof a woman bathing; and the
woman was very beautiful

As we open this chapter, I want to show you the power women possess, either on purpose or accidentally. Women have the power to change lives or whatever they encounter. So many times, women just go along with men, knowing they are wrong, just to keep the peace. But because of the power a woman has over life and death, God didn't make her to get along, but to help the man. So many men are failing today because women say things like, *"Are you sure?"* instead of *"NO,"* especially when they know the men are wrong. I know some women who do things better by accident than some people do on purpose. If the truth be told, women are superior to men. Who else do you know who can make, feed, carry, and care for the child from birth to adulthood while doing all the other things an adult is supposed to do? She does everything -- you name it, she did it; just watch her sometimes and see all that she does for you and the family. Now, you tell me who's **BAD: MJ is bad, but she's bader Hee, Hee in my Michael Jackson voice...**

I'll never forget one holiday season my wife and I made plans to travel home for Christmas to be with family. On the day we were supposed to travel, there was a storm brewing on the East Coast. It was not here yet, but on the way. I said to my wife, "Let's get to moving before the storm hits." My wife said, I don't know, the weatherman said it's bad up north. I said, *"If we leave now, we'll make it before the storm comes."*

Well, my wife said to me, "Honey, I think we should wait and see what happens first with the storm." Well, I thought that it was crazy to wait. So, I said to her, "Just get your stuff, we're going right now." She said, loudly, "No! We're not going now." I said, "Yes, we are." She said, "The devil is a lie! No, we're not. A storm is coming and I'm not going." Well, thank God for her big No, because that storm brewed into one of the biggest storms the East Coast had on record. The power that she had was in her No.

That year all up and down the East Coast people lost life, limb, and possessions. We had some friends who left North Carolina for New York a day before we had planned to leave. The trip from North Carolina to New York takes 10 or 11 hours at most. Weeks later, after they were back South we talked. They said it took them about 20 hours to get to New York that year. That was the reason they were gone for so long. If we had left at the time I wanted to go, we would have been caught smack dead in the eye of the storm. Our friends said the highway was closed when they tried to get back home. So, they had to stay a little longer before they could come home to North Carolina. Thank God my wife stood her ground with an emphatic No.

(This would have been the second time my wife saved my life. I'll tell you about the first time later in the book.)

If only Bathsheba had known the power of her no. I know David was the king and he used his power to take advantage of her, but no means no all over the world in every language. If she had said a simple no, Uriah would have lived, and the child David and Bathsheba had would not have died. That's the power of one woman.

There is absolutely, unequivocally, no doubt about why a woman is not running this country. None. A woman is, and always has been, over qualified. As quiet as its kept, women have been running things for a long time. In fact, I think, she's up to the 45th President (undocumented)... *I'm just saying*.

When I look at stories like Bathsheba's, I have to wonder how many more lives would or could have been saved if people had just learned how to say no at the right time. One of the things we do is make *choices*. God opens choices as options to live by. You get to make the choices, but you cannot control the *consequences*. You can choose to drink and drive, but you don't choose whether the consequence of your choice is an arrest or a car accident, which could lead to you killing yourself or someone else. You can choose to have sex, but not whether the consequence is an unwanted pregnancy or a sexually transmitted disease. *(Are you with me)?* A simple no can make a world of difference. I don't want for a minute to put the blame on women, but I want you to know that there is a hand that rocks the cradle, and it's a woman's hand. *"With her hands, heart, and mind, a woman can guide a child to make the right choices and those choices can lead to positive consequences"*

When you look at almost any successful man, you'll see a strong woman right by his side. It's a known fact that a man lives a longer and more successful life with a spouse. It could probably be safe to say then, that life and death are in the power of a woman. Maybe that seems like an overstatement, but I hope you understand my point. A woman can save a man's life if he works with her. How many times has a woman stopped a man from hurting or killing another man? Many times. Bathsheba could have stopped the consequences of David's senseless actions if she had used her power; the only thing David wanted was her sex, and he could have gotten that anywhere, remember he was the King. The worst thing that would have happened to a married woman denying a king would have been maybe a loss of favor in the town, but surely not death. It was against the law to be with another man's wife. It was not only frowned upon; it was punishable by death. She may have been a Hero to other women in the town --who knows? ... If she had just said No.

Remember the woman caught in the act of adultery? They wanted to stone her and even the king would have had to be mindful not to break his laws. All a woman had to do was say no. When a woman says no to a man, the whole world stands behind her, especially when it's something he wants her to do that is against her will. Unfortunately, most women don't, so when one stands up for her rights, she has superpower.

In 2003, basketball great Kobe Bryant was arrested when a woman accused him of raping her in a hotel room in Eagle, Colorado. In 2006, news broke that basketball legend Michael Jordan had been paying a woman hundreds of thousands of dollars to keep their adulterous affair secret. Oh, and let's not forget Mike Tyson we want to jail because a woman said No. All hell broke out against these two celebrated athletes. One went to jail and the other was on his way; why? All because the women said they had told these men No! after dinner and a movie. Now let's not get it twisted on what they were doing at the hotel with men with a boner, an erected penis all the time... real talk. After all, what do most men and women go to hotels and motels for?

Bathsheba could have saved her husband and her child's lives if she had used the power of no. David and Bathsheba caused all entangled in the mess they'd made to fall. Uriah died, assassinated by an out-of-control man on crack. You know *crack*. lol ... The baby boy became ill, so David prayed and fasted while the child lived. Once the child died, David rose, ate and went into the house of the Lord and opened with praise and worship. David's worship changed everything. That is the point I wanted to bring out about doing what is right: it changes things. David and Bathsheba had just come out of a horrific sin that caused at least two people to lose their lives. If *I* were the judge, jury and executioner, we would be going straight to the gallows hanging David but look at God! He dropped all the charges against them and allowed them as husband and wife, to have another child, Solomon.

Matthew 1:6 (ESV)
And Jesse the father of David the king.
And David was the father of Solomon by the
wife of Uriah

That's the power of one woman. When we do what's right, God moves on our behalf. You may say, *"Where is the right in them laying again?"* The right is doing things God's way. David was wrong interfering in Uriah's life, but he was right in being open to hearing from God and not humiliating Bathsheba's life after the fact of their adulterous relationship. God protects us even in our wrong, if we repent and turn from our evil ways. My message to you, ladies, is use your power the right way. If Bathsheba had just said no, God would have moved on her behalf, I'm sure. So, women of today, don't be scared to say no if saying no is the right action to take. God will take care of you. I don't care if he sees you on the roof bathing, or on a stripper's pole in the club, *no means no,* in every language and God will have your back.

God anointed your sex for you as a wife to have with your husband, so don't let no *(King or Queen)* take advantage of you. Use your power to save the husbands and the babies.

Let's look at another scripture:

1 Kings 19:2-3 (ESV)
"Then Jezebel sent a messenger to Elijah,
saying, "So may the gods do to me and more
also, if I do not make your life as the life of one
of them by this time tomorrow." Then he was
afraid, and he arose and ran for his life."

Here, the power of one-woman name Jezebel, she had a man running for his life. Look at the power in Jezebel's words. Elijah had just witnessed God's power -- his God's power-- and he not only ran, but he left his servants, all because of what one woman said. Jezebel had not done anything yet; she just used the power in her voice, and Elijah took flight! Now, *that's* power! ... Let's look closely at what is going on. Elijah's God had just made an open display of power in front of the 450 men who were following Baal, "the devil..." God showed up, and not only did God consume the burnt, sacrificed wood and stone, he licked up all the water in the trench. With the help of his God, Elijah executed -- slaughtered -- all of them. Elijah's God had just done all this for him, but soon after, he was running from one woman because she promised to do the same thing he had just did to the 450 men he just slaughter! -- Women, take note and remember how powerful you are if you use that power for the right reason. Despite seeing the fire of the living God consume the godly sacrifice at Mt. Carmel, Ahab the King still listened to his wife. You would think Ahab would be convinced by Elijah's God, but no; he listened to his wife: one woman. *Now, that's powerful, whether good or bad.*

When a woman puts her foot down, all the earth recognizes it. Look at Mother Nature, who commands attention in almost every season. The power of one woman can bring Kings down and put them on the run. So, don't sell yourself cheap because God favors you, you're his highest expression in the earth, a Masterpiece. Ahab was the king and wore the crown, but his wife worked and had power over the throne; she ran the business. *That's powerful!*

Let's look at one scripture where Jesus saved two he loved, one about a girl restored to life, and the other about a woman healed:

Matthew 9:18-20 (ESV)
A ruler came in and knelt before him, saying,
'My daughter has just died, but come and lay
your hand on her, and she will live.' ...
And behold, a woman who had suffered from
a discharge of blood for twelve years *came*
up behind him and touched the
fringe of his garment..."

Now, God is showing His love not for just one person; He's doubling up on his love for his children, both female in these scriptures. When the ruler -- Jairus was his name -- came to Jesus, he told Jesus that his daughter had just died. Jesus said go away, for the girl is not dead, but sleeping, isn't it funny what we see as die, *God sees as sleeping.* In another instance, when Jesus heard that Lazarus had died, He *wept.* He was coming to him, *but with delay.* He waited an extra day before going to see about Lazarus, but not for his daughters in these scriptures. When He heard that Jairus's daughter had just died, He moved *immediately.* Ladies, that's a good place to give God some praise. Isn't it ironic how in one situation He cries, but in another He makes haste? That's the love He has for his daughters. I believe there's a special place in God's heart for women, so much so that when He created Adam, the Bible says that even though He created male and female at the same time in the beginning, in Genesis chapter 1, woman didn't come on the scene until Genesis chapter 2, when everything was all in place and ready for her. This text may not sound like much, but it is, because everyone cries when a loved one dies. But how many come to see about you immediately?

Just one: the one and only God. That's how much God thinks of you.

Genesis 1:27 (ESV)
So, God created man in his own image,
in the image of God, he created him;
male and female.

~Genesis 2:22 (ESV)
"And the rib that the Lord God had taken from
the man he made into a woman.... "

If you look closely into these scriptures, you'll see that God favors you in so much that He made sure everything was ready, in place first before you came on the scene. So, ladies before you hook up with some Bozo, auditioning for *(Ringing Brothers Circus),* made sure he is not in fact some clown on the run. Trust me there's a lot of them out there! Then make sure he has everything ready for you, if nothing else make sure he loves God because if he loves God, he'll take care of you.

Women you are so special to God, that he put Adam on the earth first by himself to make sure the coast was clear for you to come and live on earth safely, making sure the animals had their names and were under control first. When you're in trouble He comes immediately to see about you. Who can ask for anything more? Consider the power of one woman. Even the Master comes running on her behalf. In Matthew 9:20, watch how the Master respond to one of his daughters, and what she said to herself.

Matthew 9:20-22 (ESV)
And behold, a woman who had suffered from
a discharge of blood for twelve years came
up behind him and touched the fringe of his
garment, said to herself, "If I only touch his
garment, I will be made well.

Some theologians say that for this woman to touch the hem of His garment, she had to crawl on her knees to make her way through the crowd. Jesus was on his way to restore the life of a little girl and a woman crawled up to him and touched His garment. Jesus faced two crises at the same time, but it wasn't too much for the Master to take care of them both. Jesus didn't talk with the woman about her problem; all He knew was that she was in need, and He made her well. For all He knew, she could've been a stumbling drunk. Praise the Lord for his faithfulness! Wherever Jesus finds you, up or down, crawling or walking, He can and will make you whole. Remember, the woman was crawling to Jesus, and He healed her on credit, knowing she would praise him later. That is another example of the power of one woman, to get things done on credit a real I-O-U. Women, instead of crawling to some man, you should start crawling to Jesus; because wherever and however He finds you, He will leave you whole. Look at God.

Let's look at leprosy and the significance of Jesus making a woman *(whole)* from it. I have two refence scriptures, Matthew 9:22 & Luke 17:19 please read. Now listen, in the Bible days, leprosy was a disease that attacks the nervous system, and people would lose limbs, ears, nose, fingers; (literally) whatever part of the body the disease attacked, you would lose that part of your body. There was no cure outside of the (Master Jesus) so it was almost a death sentence. I'm not saying this woman had that disease, what I'm saying is Jesus made her whole. I don't know what issues she struggled with prior to finding Jesus. All I know is Jesus, our Lord and savior, bypassed her issues and met every need. *I can do a dance on that alone... Smile.* Jesus not only wants to make you well or heal your sickness, but Jesus came and made her **whole,** which means. He left her with nothing lacking or broke; He left her *complete.* He wants to give you everything back that the devil stole from you, past and present. I like the way God thinks about us.

Ladies read Proverbs 18:22 to your man or encourage him to read it. The King James version is especially powerfully written. Tell your man that I said that scripture is a game changer. Read it! I'll break it down for him! Look how God set us up, and hook the woman up right in the process:

Proverbs 18:22 (KJV)
*Whoso findeth a wife findeth a good thing,
and obtaineth favour of the LORD.*

Here is some free advice for men: if you want to be blessed, find yourself a wife and treat her well. Marriage is sanctified and holy; sacred even. It is where all your favor is stored. There have been a lot of times that I failed in life because I didn't know what was expected of me, but this one thing I can't fail at because it is right in front of me. She was even once a part of me disguised as a Rib. I'm happy – yes, I am -- because I think I found the *(Genie in the bottle).* All we must do now is follow the instructions in the book, (the bible) because this is a game changer.

Now the penalties for not being a lady first are on the man because now you know what's expected of you, we have the cheat sheet right in the front of us, so now we have no excuses to fail this test. All we must do, guys, is find a wife and treat her right -- that sounds easy -- and the favor of God will be in your life, just like that you'll be set for life. Ladies, you are so powerful that mankind's **blessings are housed inside of you.** Getting to those blessings is all based on a man finding you and loving you, and your man is favored by God. Guys, they not only carry babies, but they are also carrying our destiny. That is God's favor. I don't know about other men but count me in and *super-size it.* Smile...That is the power of one woman.

Look at what else God's word tells us.

1 Peter 3:7 (ESV)
"Likewise, husbands, live with your wives in
an understanding way, showing honor to the
woman as the weaker vessel, so that your
PRAYERS MAY NOT BE HINDERED."

What a kick in the pants: if you want your prayers answered, honor your lady. That's right all the prayers you prayed run through your wife to God. *(Great ball of fire).* It's right there in black and white, in the word of God. *Don't say I never gave you nothing.* That woman you're mistreating or loving holds your success in this life; yup! that little So and So, (smile)... that's everything, she holds your favor and determines if your prayers will be answered on time. I want God to hear my prayers, so

I'm going to treat my wife even better than I already do so my prayers are not hindered (made slow or difficult). Gentlemen, our wives, girlfriends, boo have got the goods to all our blessings from God. There is a penalty for all of us if we sin: the wages of sin is death. To make it simple, remember that playing your woman **cheap** can cost you everything.

Romans 6:23 (ESV)
"For the wages of sin is death, but the gift of God is eternal *life in Christ Jesus our Lord.*"

Look how close women are to blessing our lives; the power they wield is almost like Christ's. People of God, we really need to look at this gift God has given man in the form of a woman, who was once a rib in our side, what's better: being blessed by God or having the favor of God? Although they sound like one in the same, I do know that *"he who finds a wife, finds a good thing and obtains favor from the Lord"* this is how God set it up for men to receive blessings from their wives. Guys get on your game and get things right with the love of your life. Gentlemen get your Blessing back with your favor, woman.

Let's look at another example of the power of one woman in the word of God. *This Sista is off the hook.*

2 Kings 4:26 (ESV)
"Is all well with the child?" And she answered, "All is well."

This scripture comes from a story about a Shunamite woman whose son died on her lap. After his death, the father asked about the boy's whereabouts. The woman never said, "the boy just died on my lap and he's in the other room dead on the bed". She says to her husband, *"All IS WELL."*

Who does that? This woman was a woman of faith and power, that loved and believed God for everything. She also was a wealthy woman that would house and feed Elisha on his travel, that how this whole thing started. The Shunamite woman's son has just died and she's telling people and her husband that all is well. This woman's action showed her strong faith, despite her overwhelming sorrow. She placed the fate of her son back on the man of God whose Word and by the means of God's mercy she had gained her son in the first place. This woman gave the boy back to the man that prophesied that she would have a child. This is a teachable moment; because this woman had enough sense to bring her problems back to the man who gave them to her. *(Lord, help us to bring all our problems and troubles back to you.)* This woman not only brought her problems back to the prophet, she also covered up the death. The power of this woman comes from her faith that if she could get back to the Lord, like the woman with the issue of blood, everything would be all right. Even in the face of her son's death, this Shunamite woman declares, *"all is well"* at one of the worst times in her life. Look at the scenario for a moment, the pain she felt because of the death of her child was worse than the emptiness she'd felt before he was born. She had wanted a child, but she had never asked for one. The prophet wanted to bless her womb, for giving him a place to stay in his travels and for being so kind to him. She was fine without a child because her husband was old, and God did not give them one. (*You must read all on free time), 2 Kings 4:8-37.*

So, to have a child on someone else's word, only to lose the child, would cause unimaginable pain, but nevertheless, she made her way to the man of God saying, *"all is well"* and God gave the child new life again. Boy, she is tuff!

Regardless of the overwhelming circumstances, God is still able to save us. All we must do is believe. Just remember the power is in you.

This woman's simple declaration, of *"all is well,"* activated her faith and the child who was dead came back to life. That's shouting music all by itself, the power of one woman. Now fella can you see why you must find a lady and treat her right. *FYI: you will never be above your confession, she'll get you there.*

Most people, finding themselves in such a situation, would have been screaming, crying, running around the house, or yelling. But this Shunamite woman declared, "all is well." I like her attitude about her loss, because facing the reality of her son's was no easy task, so certainly her expectation that he would be coming back to life was even more unimaginable. Such unshakable faith is the foundation in *Mark 5:40,* when Jesus put the doubters out of the house when He brought the little girl back to life:

Mark 5:40 (ESV)
"He put them all outside"

If you are ever going to do anything great, you must first have the right attitude about it, and then you must put the **doubters out**-- not just the ones in your house, but the ones in your head, also. When Lazarus, the brother of Mary and Martha, died and Jesus brought him back to life, it was because the sisters had the right attitude and believed God in the person of Jesus, the miracle man who brings people back to life. So how did the Shunamite woman turn things around? She relied solely on her faith in God and the power she possessed. The Shunamite woman knows who she belongs to.

All throughout history, women were the backbone and sometimes the spine for men, especially in the African American churches. One church I attended was 75% plus women, so let's not try to debate on that fact! We need to recognize that fact and stop being so *"macho."* I think we men can turn this whole thing around by just telling the truth. We never would have made it without *strong women*. Sometimes women have to be there not just for the man, but for the whole family. When the truth replaces the lies, old or new, the structure will stand, in other words *(clean up, what you messed up)*. Buildings stand because they have strong infrastructures, the underlying foundation or basic framework of any building, system, or organization, whether they are, skyscraper big or small. Most infrastructures are never seen, but the bigger the building, the stronger the infrastructure, that enable them to withstand earthquakes up to a certain level on the Richter scale. Most women, if not all, have been the infrastructure -- the underlying support system -- of good and bad men. *(Remember she was the first infrastructure, known as the Rib)*. I've seen it growing up in the hood, men living low lives with good women and she would build him up to do great things and start to believe in himself. This is my opinion! It's time to just put the truth in the right places and give the never-seen infrastructure *(woman)* her due.

I'm fascinated with women's strength and how they stand even in adversity. *(Women, in some ways are like tea bags: you'll never know how strong they really are until you put them in hot water).* I've seen it with my own eyes. My momma did it for years in the projects. That topic is too sensitive for me to go into detail; but I will say this: just because someone claims to be your friend doesn't stop that person from hurting you. Growing up was fun and hard at the sometime but never the less, I'm glad to be here writing this book free and in my right mind. Women just have inner strength men don't have or understand, I still don't know why the bible calls her the weaker vessel with all that she does.

When my son and I would get sick, my wife nurses us back to health. On the other hand, when she gets sick, the whole house is down until she gets back on her feet. My wife can bring the whole house back to life. That's the power of one woman and that's what we need to recognize: she has the power, in some regards, to heal the sick and raise the dead. *You don't hear me!* Women have power for your structure to stand in her infrastructure,

Remember, she holds your favor. Look at some of what favor means: endowed with special advantages or gifts or having preferential treatment. Man, that alone is enough to make me want to find a good thing -- a Woman -- and treat her right. I want to show you another famous woman in the Bible. We find her in Joshua 2.

Joshua 2:4 (ESV)
"But the woman had taken the two men and hidden them..."

She had a special way with men. Her name was Rahab. *Yes Ray-Ray.* She was a prostitute in Jericho who helped Joshua's spies hide and escape Jericho. After exploring and letting them hide on her roof, when the Israelites captured Jericho, they spared the house with the scarlet cord in the window. That cord was a sign that a friend of God's people lived there. Rahab was, therefore, both a prostitute and a *friend of God!* Regardless of her title, the power of this one woman was that she had the ability to save lives. Her mother, father, brothers and all her father's household were spared for what she had done.

If she had gotten caught, her whole family would've been wiped off the planet. They would kill kids and everybody, down to a few generations. What Rahab did take guts because if the spies had been caught in her house, she and the spies and all her family would have been either hung, killed, or thrown in the lion's den for a snack.

I'm telling you, if you want to live a long life, find a wife and treat her right.

Rahab single-handedly saved the whole family, along with the spies she was protecting. Now that's power. In fact, Rahab was the wife of Solomon according to the genealogy of Jesus Christ.

Matthew 1:6 (ESV)
And David was the father of Solomon
by the wife of Uriah,

Their son Boaz married Ruth and became the father of Obed, the grandfather of Jesse and the great grandfather of David a Canaanite *"harlot" Rahab* became part of the lineage of King David; out of which the Messiah came. Talk about favor; and the power of one woman. Wow, a woman, good or bad has the power to hook you up with the Master Jesus Christ; a sign that God's grace and forgiveness is extended to all. What I'm saying is that God's love is not limited by nationality or the nature of a person's sin. *Boy oh boy,* I'll never look down on a **Ho** again, I mean a lady of the night. Smile... The scriptures do not tell us how Rahab, who came out of a culture where harlotry and adultery were acceptable, she somehow recognized the Lord as the one, true God. Her insight recorded in Joshua leaves no doubt that she did so. This Canaanite woman's declaration of faith led the writers of the epistles in the book of Hebrew to cite Rahab as one of the heroes of faith.

Hebrews 11:31 (ESV)
"By faith Rahab the prostitute did not perish
with those who were disobedient, because she
had given a friendly welcome to the spies."

The book of James also commended her as an example of one who had been justified by works.

James 2:25 (ESV)
...was not also Rahab the prostitute
justified by works..."

What an amazing woman. There is one more thing I researched about Rahab, according to *(Rabbinic tradition),* Rahab was one of the foremost beautiful women in the world and was the ancestor of eight prophets including Jeremiah and the prophetess *Huldah,* who is mentioned in the Hebrew Bible in 2 Kings 22:14-20 and 2 Chronicles 34:22-28. *Be careful about how you speak of people, because you don't know who you could be talking about. (Say Amen).*

All our lives we try to do good, and don't make it to the hall of fame. This harlot got her freak on and made it to the canons of the apostle's writings all the way to the heroes of faith. Now that's the power of one extraordinary woman. *Get your freak on, and go Big time, go ray-ray. (go ray ray)* ...

It doesn't even feel right referring to Rahab as a harlot. She should be called a woman who worked for God. I have a lot of respect for her whorish ways; and the lie she told. Can lying be an acceptable course of action? And was that Godly? You be the judge. I think we should honor Rahab the way the Bible does and see the power of one woman from all angles. In all respects, women have it going on. I just think it's time to salute them and stop holding up their progress.

I was on my job one day and some of the stylists were talking among themselves about working long hours and getting home late. One of the women complained to the higher-ups about the long hours. This company had been operating with the same hours for decades. The workers spoke to the shop supervisor, but their concerns fell on deaf ears. One day, the district supervisor was visiting the salon and the same stylists spoke with her about the work schedule, conditions, and having little family time. Without a meeting or appointments, and with no paperwork, the district supervisor went into the shop supervisor's office for about five or ten minutes and changed the shop hours. That's the power of one woman.

The store hours remained still the same, but the shop hours changed to one hour less all over the country. That's a huge accomplishment. This woman – a worker, not a supervisor -- had no meetings or appointments, changed the way a corporation was run in a few minutes in one day.

All women have this amazing power. I know it was a woman thing because women are moms from the time their feet hit the floor and she knew it and knew what other women were going through; working long hours and still having to take care of their families. In a matter of minutes, one woman changed the way a multi-billion-dollar business was run. Men, we must catch up and stop being last on giving our women top flight *(Aretha Franklin) R-E-S-P-E-C-T* and recognition.

I'm telling you one thing, if you want news or dirt about what's happening on the dark side of town, go to a prostitute's house. And if you want to meet Jesus, go to a prostitute's house. That statement may not sound right, but, in Rahab's case, it's the truth. Never count anyone out when it comes to Jesus saving him or her; especially a woman. She might be the very one to save your life. And please get the metaphor right for going to a prostitute's house for whatever reasons. She really may have the power to save the lives of you and your family members. Never in my wildest dreams would I think a prostitute would save lives the way Rahab did, let alone save souls. Well she did, and that's *the power of one woman.* I almost feel like I'm cheating her with such a short chapter in this book. I feel like there's so much more to say about

Rahab. If I had one thing to say about Rahab the lady, it would be may your spirit live forever.

Chapter 5

Victoria Has A Secret;
So, Should You

Psalm 27:5 (ESV)
"For in the time of trouble he shall
hide me in his pavilion: in the 'secret'
of his tabernacle shall he hide me;"

I would love to share some things with you that I learned about the secret places and things that are close and dear to me as well as special and dear to God's word, like when he called the *'Pavilion' the secret place.* There is a special place that is designed for us; God's people, that we need to learn more about. Not only does He keep us from troubles, He keeps trouble from us as well. Small for some, but huge when the Bible said were trouble on every side.

2 Corinthians 4:8 (ESV)
We are afflicted in every way, but not crushed;
perplexed, but not driven to despair;

While God is trying to keep us from the enemy's attacks, some of us are showing all what God is trying to keep hidden from the enemy. Showing all your goods to the world was not God's plan for our lives. He calls it the **secret place** for a reason. "Hidden" means to keep from knowledge or view. If God is trying to keep certain things from view, why are we so excited to show what He clearly is trying to keep a secret? When I thought about Victoria and her secret, when I started to write this chapter, the first thing that came to my mind, with **Victoria's secret,** was woman in teddies and thongs. You know the kind of women's underpants that has only a thin strip of material in the back that shows everything except for the split. Wow, that intro alone got my mouth wet. Excuse me, I'm the writer and I see way into this secret place. This is what I'm talking about with the secret place allowing people to see extra parts of you is letting the cat out of the bag, so to speak. So, He not only has to keep our mind from troubles, but our physical bodies as well. How did I get that out of the *"pavilion"* or the *"secret place"* is beyond me, keep reading to see where I'm going with this "secret place"? When I think about all the money people put into this little piece of material and call it a secret, you would think it would be a secret as small as it is, but no, it's a billion-dollar secret that men pay for. Well, **I guess the secret is out**. For a long time, I wanted to know about *Victoria's secret,* not just the garment, I get that! but the Real secret. I wanted to know why men spend Billions for sex when God gave the woman to man for free to love and honor, but for some crazy reason we, I mean (he) still want to pay.

Genesis 2:22 (ESV)
And the rib that the Lord God had taken from
the man, He made into a woman and brought
her to the man.

That's the secret. Ladies, Victoria has a secret so should you. After viewing and ponding my research of Victoria, the verdict is out. Ladies when you reveal your private information, (parts) the challenge or pursuit is off for the pursuer, *(do you hear the words, that are coming out of my mouth)*? Because he now knows where you are, and it's no fun chasing something or someone when you already know the location they are in; now he just pays for it because the thrill is gone. So, Victoria called it a secret for you to figure out. I want to encourage you to get back to your secret place, not just from trouble, insecurity or uncertainty, but to the place of security in the things of God. Our text reads,

"for in the time of trouble he shall hide me in his pavilion: in the secret of his tabernacle shall he hide me;

In today's world, the cigarette commercial coins a phrase that says, *"You've come a long way baby!"* Well it's deteriorating. Why? ...because there was a time when women worked together to make sure her sister girl was treated fairly and properly by others and their sorority stayed tight maintaining the love and respect for one another. There was a time when women would get together with other women talking about nothing... well, not *"nothing,"* but you know what I mean, and had fun doing it; going shopping, to the movies or malls, hair, nails, etc.... keeping their secret strong, whatever they were doing it worked. When you see women together today talking or too close holding hands, you don't know what to think. That was how women related back then; working on their secret. Now, people are trying to figure it out, they don't know what's going on and the secret is losing its sauce. In my opinion woman are struggling with their identity, no fault of their own. Victoria has a secret so should you. There's a saying, *"never let your left hand know what your right hand is doing."* This brings me to my next point, Boy! I'm going to get into trouble down at the gym when the boys hear about this. A lady should never, ever-ever let or tell a man you're a virgin or I'm waiting until marriage for sex, *that's a no-no,* because once a man finds that out about you, your cooked, done. We can stick a fork in you, you're done. (really)... FYI, We, can wait forever to be the first one to crack that egg. (So, to speak). Not only that, you just put a bullseye on your back in bold letters, saying please come take advantage of me. I can't tell you why, but it's the truth. I'm already in enough trouble down at the gym with the boys, (will maybe I can tell you). We, I mean he love new on touch tight form fitting relation... please don't look at me different you asked, once he knows that about you, he will pursue you or sit on you like a hen on an egg or a chicken on a chick waiting on you to hatch or crack! ...not all, but most. So, when a man approaches you the wrong way about your personal information, instead of saying, *"I'm waiting for marriage before sex,"* just say *"hell to the no,* I'm not interested in having sex with your nasty... because if you don't hold your ground, you will be played like the card game *spades, with a lot of hits, and end up busted.* So, ladies please keep your secrets, because (ladies and virgins) are hard to find, according to scripture.

Proverbs 31:10 (ESV)
An excellent wife who can find?
She is far more precious than jewels.

Somebody please tell me how far is far? Dict:*(A great distance in space or time.)* This is the love God has for you, ladies… To Infinity and beyond! (That was a freebee). There was a time when you could find a virgin at the tender age of twenty or twenty-five, now she might be in her teens or tweens… too soon, really? That's a shame. Ladies you must get back to your secrets, not trickery, but female information (girl talk), and keep a lady's information on the need to know basis and who's who, and what's going on with "who." This is a special interest of mine for two reasons. First, my mother is a woman, and second, I have four sisters and a host of nieces; so, it's time for mankind to really be our brother's keeper. Brother, sister, you name it, (just help) … it's time to look out for one another, especially when the ones that are supposed to keep the peace are shooting men in the back running unarmed, it's time to go back to the way the slaves made it from the south to the north, by keeping the secrets sacred amount the *"brother/ Sista hood."* Oh yes, it's time! I interrupted two ladies talking one day, and the ladies politely excused me and said, *"This is girl's talk,"* and went on talking like I was not even in the room. That's part of the secret keeping the guidelines safe and knowing who you let in your conversation. The godfather of soul MR. James Brown sung a song, entitled, **"it's a man's world,"** but it would be nothing without a woman. Now there's two ways to look at this, was Brown saying women should stay in their place or just fill in where needed? *Either way, this world would be* *absolutely (nothing) without a woman!* Ladies, that alone lets the world know you are favored by God, but until you stand your ground, not with gun's like coward's killing innocent people I might add, (God people) … but with the dominion power inside of you. God made you with a purpose in mind, humanity would be nothing without you! The word of God declares that there is a secret place, and unlike some men, reneging on their promises, God is a promise keeper and He keeps his word concerning you. Look what, 1 Corinthians 2:9 has to say about the secret place:

1 Corinthians 2:9 (ESV)
But, as it is written, "What no eye has seen, nor ear heard, nor the heart of man imagined, what God has prepared for those who love him"—

We may never know or discover the mysteries of God or the full benefits of Christ death in our understanding, but God is the same today, yesterday, and forevermore. If where ever going to be successful in relationships, we must get back to the Creator mindset for men and women original design and inherent makeup. The same goes for the secret place, yes, God is our savior and our help in the time of trouble, even in that He doesn't show us everything. Ladies with that said, there is something special about you, and your lifestyle is your secret; like how much money you have in the bank, or what you like to do when you're with your lover. Some things are none of other people's business when it comes to your lifestyle; it's your good and bad secrets. The worst thing you can do getting to know people, is letting them know too much about you too soon; where you live, work, rest or play is your personal space, *(Do I need to say that again)?* so watch how much you give up (both ways), real talk.... I think the thing I'm trying to say is women on a whole should be very careful how they give up information to others. I know that's not how we communicate today, that I know, but once you give up some of the right information to the wrong person you just let the world into your world or your secret space, (you heard) really... and I don't think that's what you meant to do. So, remember Victoria has a secret so should you. When we go to the doctor and give them your personal information, they can pull up almost anything about us, literally... Everywhere you go today they want your email address, it seems more important than your street address to where you live; so, watch what you reveal for all intents purposes because they will send you *junk mail* either way business or personal. That's just what happens when you give up your secret or personal information to the wrong person, you get '**junk man**'... I mean mail. The same goes for the internet or cyberspace, once your Info; is out there you can forget about it. The secret or info you just gave up allows people to come in and out of your life whenever they want. (that was a mouth full) ... Now you know that isn't right. So, Victoria calls here's a secret, well said. Ladies Victoria has a secret so should you. There's a secret place and it's for your protection, most horror movies have a plot were someone in the story exposes the friend to the killer, and somehow gave up important information and the killer follows them to their secret place; home! the place he was never supposed to know about. I saw it once in the "movies." How did he find out? ...someone gave up important "free" information to your whereabouts; and now there's a crime, (did I go too far)? Smile... What I'm saying to the ladies is that your secret place is your secret, all the way down to where you go shopping or playing. Your personal information is a huge part of your identity, so that brings me back to the picture you paint. When you dress up, remember what Flip Wilson said in his comedy when he dressed up as Geraldine Jones: *"What you see is what you get!"* Now you don't have to dress up like Moms Mabley *(she was an old school comedian before Flip, and dress real homely like),* to keep your secrets, but you should never dress up with the intention to sell. You need to remember; your dress code is a huge part of your identity in this world. Be very careful what you show or sale in your dress code, believe me, your dress code says a lot to a man. When you wear certain things, our mind goes around the world and we never left the room. Really… Sometimes your dress code can get you into trouble, to the point where some guys just *"take"* what they see. I didn't say take sex, I'm just reporting the news. It's not your fault, but if I were you, I would show it, but to the *"one"* I adore, not the *"one's."* Guys are visual, and they have it honestly. That doesn't give them the right to touch or take what they see without permission. In the beginning, God gave Adam a big job and let him name all the animals according to what he saw, and still today men are naming things by what they see.

Genesis 2:19 (ESV)
Now out of the ground the Lord God had
formed every beast of the field and every bird
of the heavens and brought them to the man
to see what he would call them. And whatever
the man called every living creature,
that was its name.

In the past men were good name callers, but lately he's not as good as he once was. When you watch music videos and some **gangsta rap,** he has all kinds of names for you -- new ones-- so watch what you show, because he will tell or name it; good or bad, he's going to give it a name. Therefore, the word of God says, *"eyes have not seen."* Some things are just your secret, and for the eyes of your (one and only) man or woman. You can't show all your stuff to people, especially little boys; big or small. We tell everything. Why do you think all of what you did with him is all over town? Have you ever thought of that? not just concerning your dress code, but about life in general? When you show people your ideas or things you're planning on doing, some people will try to steal your **million-dollar invention or idea from you.** That's what's been happening to women every day showing their stuff to people with bad intentions; especially Mr. Wrong. He has been stealing dreams ideas and breaking hearts on a regular, because you showed your secret to the wrong person and he took advantage of you. So, ladies, if you want to keep the advantage, show less, and watch him give you more; that's right more of him and all his possessions. *(I know that I'm talking about)* ... My (wife) is the boss. Victoria has a secret so should you. There was a lady in the word of God that was a harlot, a prostitute that kept a secret and hid the spies, and because of that her name is in the Hall of Fame in the Kingdom of God. Eve, on the other hand, the first woman that had a secret, exposed it and fell, her and Adam. Rahab kept her secret and want bigtime in the bible.

Joshua 2:6 (ESV)
But she had brought them up to the roof and
hid them with the stalks of flax that she had
laid in order on the roof.

What I'm trying to say is your secrets are valuable to your success in this life. God doesn't care where you come from or your background in life. He just wants to bless you.

James 1:19 (ESV)
Hearing and Doing the Word. Know this, my
beloved brothers: let every person be quick to
hear, slow to speak, slow to anger;

I think God, gave us two ears to hear more and one mouth to say less. What you think? When you master your emotions, you're not quick to show all your important things, like cars, home, and investments. Some things you just don't show. Getting to know people is a lifetime journey. Meeting someone at a club one night and showing them all your stuff is a setback for women hundreds of years as far as relationships goes when men are concerned, and in (general). So, hold your secret long as you can, never lie or cheat, but never- ever give up your personal information for free.

Quick story... My son and I were out shopping one day, and a lady said to me, "Is this your son? He's cute." I said to her, "Thank you, they say he looks like daddy." I went on to say, I have four boys in all." I unknowing just gave up free info. All she said to me was "he's cute." *(That one son I was with)*. She didn't ask me how many kids I have. I voluntarily gave her that information for free. She could've been the female killer for all I knew. That's what I mean about keeping your secret, not lies, but that's my personal business sir or ma'am. So, if you think a man is going to invest in you after a one-night stand and knowing all your secrets, you are so out of touch with the way guys think or operate. This is not cute to say, but the average guy will screw a rock once the light is out; some with the lights on. Smile... --I told you it's not nice to say, but it's the truth. If the ladies God gave us to dwell with are going to have staying power or a fighting chance in the wifey roll, the intimate thing about you are going to have to stay between you and your man, not men. Yes, the man God blessed you with. You know most guys can't keep a secret 24 hours when it comes to strange *'pussy cat'*... Oh boy, I know I'm getting kicked out of the boy's club and the church for saying that, but guys tell everything connected to them. We say woman are gossipers, that may be true, but guys are big talkers, you know like, I did this, or I did that, or I own this, or my family is so-and-so, or my father is *Mr. Universe... not Mr. America, but World...* We put things way up there, Moms, maybe Wifey, business may be off limits, but girlfriend down is public information. Notice I said wifey, "maybe." because when the relationship hit the rocks, we let it go, that's right we do tell all... I know some secrets about my wife I know I'm carrying to my grave, because now her secrets are now our secrets. Some people in fair weather relationships tell everything, but I would bet you my wife still has plenty of secrets I don't know about because it's her secret. (I get it) ... ... I hear some guys say I know all my wife secrets, (I say), you may know all the secrets she wants you to know about, please don't be no fool or get it twisted women have good secrets, trust me on that! Ladies, Victoria has a secret so should you. That's not to say she's not truthful, but who besides God knows everything about you; *no one.* Ladies, your secret is the key to your success, so be careful and mindful that what you show and tell strangers. Make sure your story has a future connected to it when you tell it or show it, because it could be the end for you in that town. (really)... *Victoria has a secret so should you.* To reiterate; 1 Corinthians 2:9.

Therefore, eyes have not seen, nor ears heard, nor has entered the heart of man the things God has prepared for those who love him;

Ladies, as we consider this text, one of the things is evidently clear to the sight and mind is that there is something untold. Would it be fair to say that God, the creator of the universe has secrets? There are some things that have not been revealed to man because it's a secret, some things you're just not ready for. Therefore, you just can't show all your stuff to people.

I like the way Jack Nicholson said it in the movie *"Officer and a Gentleman,"* when he said, *"You can't handle the truth!"* to one of the offices indicating no matter what level you're on, some things are none of your business; and ladies, that's just where I'm going some things are none of his business. It's your secret place so every Tom, Dick, Harry and Joe don't need to know all about your dirty little secrets. There's something special even life changing about our dark places like before a seed can grow into anything it first must go in the ground or dark place, the secret place is where it makes its jump from unseen into the seen or from darkness to light. I'm not implying you must die like the seed, and germinate to grow, but your secret place has the same power as a seed. Your *germinating* time or your secret place is causing you to sprout and develop into the woman, or person that God call you to be. That's why you can't tell all your secrets while you're germinating because that's what causes a seed to grow and be strong. (This is good to me). Smile... Ladies don't let anyone forfeit your growth. That's the time you're growing stronger in your dark places. So, tell him and them to leave you alone while you're growing. Most people forfeit their success giving up too much free information. (Like I did earlier with my 4 boys) telling all my beeswax. Remember, your secrets is the *"secret sauce"* that makes you unique. This was the one thing that made Victoria special it was her secrets. Now she's undeniably special and she's branded her way into America's heart from the buttock to the tune of Billions of dollars; and that's **no secret.** America is still trying to figure out what's the big deal with women's panties. That's the power of dark places and secrets it can take you to the top overnight.

Another unique phenomenon of dark or secret places is the life of the caterpillars. Before it becomes a beautiful butterfly it's a worm. Oh, bless his name!... I'm going somewhere with this. The caterpillar goes into a cocoon, a dark place, it's his secret the low places in the ground. If the worm was to let every insect know about his secret, he might never make it to the sky ants would eat him alive, especially the red ants, them suckers hurt. That's just what's happening to some woman, letting their secret out too soon, some guys eat them alive before they get their strength to fly. Like Superman before he gets into his flying suit he goes into the phone booth, back room, etc...that's his secret place. This secret place for Superman is a very special place. If he's ever going to touch the sky and do only what the man of steel can do he must go into this dark place. If we're ever going to reach our God given potential, you must spend quality time with the Master in your secret place. The low places in your life now can change overnight, just like the caterpillar when you keep your secret between you and your God. Remember, Victoria has a secret, so should you. When you think about secrets it sounds like you're hiding something, but you're not your protecting something, *(your future)*. When you look at most great entities, you never see the hard work they put in before you see their greatness. Like me writing this book was hard work. Business, corporations, churches, universities, it's hard work, you never see how they became great, like a professional athlete, we see them on TV on game night fine-tuned with special gifts, but you never see the hard work and long hours they put in missing shots, lifting weights, running, crying, giving blood sweat and tears, in the gymnasium, in the weight room, up early in the morning and on a strict diet... that's their secret place. What I'm beginning to understand is everybody has a secret place, just like the caterpillar he's great and flying high now as the beautiful butterfly, but we didn't see it in the secret place going through growing pains, that's why the secret place is so special it's a time you get to develop into greatness. So, from now on ladies it's a need-to-know basis with you know who... and how does the information you want from me help me to fly high.

Recap: Remember Secrets no lies, lies will come back and bite you, but secrets are valuable to your success. Jesus, my Lord and your savior, even had secrets. On several occasions, he would help people and say go and tell no one. Why? ...because it was his secret. In other words, it's a time for everything, and now was not the time to tell his business. Ladies if Jesus had a secret for an appointed time, so should you. *(girl, you need to tweet that) smile...* can you tell I'm having fun writing... One of the things that happen when information is released before its time is it doesn't have the same effect, like someone's *surprise birthday party.* If the person finds out before the party time, the element of the surprise is gone; and the surprise is a flop. All the fun is gone out of the person coming home to a waiting room of people, to say "Surprise!" The element of surprise is gone, and the fun is snatch out. Will the same goes with your secret, when a man knows all about your secrets, he's now going along with the fun for the ride, but the surprise is over and all the elements. FYI, the *(elements)* are the main ingredients to your success. So, ladies, if you want to stay on top of your game, don't tell lies to advance the relationship, and never tell your secrets if you want to be successful in it. Here's a bit of old school advice: keep your panties up and your dress down until the right time like the caterpillar in its dark place and your relationship will take off, why? Because sex changes the relationship two way good and bad, and when sex lead in a relationship you never know what you're going to get first, *(a baby or a ring)* trust me it's a hard gamble that you can't afford to bet on. When you give up your game changing (stuff) whatever it is, make sure he or she's has some skin in the game for good. People will hurt you intentionally or not pain hurts either way. Now, just for the record I'm not talking about harming anyone in any way, but there a place, a secret place, that's for you and your Boo; not for everybody on the streets. Your secrets house your identity, which that make you who you are, and different from the others: your own DNA. What is a secret? A secret is confidential, classified, and private. It's not that you're hiding something; it's your personal information to use at your own discretion, for your benefit.

Everyone has some sort of secret. I'm a *bootleg cook*. I love to cook. One day back home at church we had a big Christmas dinner and I was the fried chicken and beans man. I must say my chicken and beans were to live for. One of the ladies asked me, "Elder T, what do you put in your food? Because it tastes so good!" And like a fool I told her. She on the other hand would make macaroni and cheese, pork shoulders and some good Spanish rice that was also to live for. I asked her what her recipe was. Do you know what she said to me after I told her my recipe? She said, *"If I tell you, I have to kill you."* Lol... Talk about secrets! Some women have them secrets all the way down to baking a cake. (man!) ... You must keep your secret, because sometimes that's the little unknown information that might seal the deal and make you the next whatever. Ladies, in this life you should be *"whoop there she is,"* not *"whoop there it is."* A man should always put a handle on your name, you're not an it, you're a she a lady; God's Masterpiece; a gift to the world, not just mankind. Ladies your secret should demand a handle. When a lady presents herself in public she should be flawless, faultless, beautiful, and confident. When a woman shows that, you're now in a man's head; not his lower parts, you're in his head big, and now he's forming an opinion about you and that's your secret, his opinion. His imagination is going wild. Now the chase is on. It's up to you how long the chase goes. If you lay down too fast and give up your secret, the chase is over, I think BB King said it best in one of his hit songs, *"The thrill is gone."* Ladies, your secret is maximizing the longer you can keep Victoria's panties on your back. Seriously, people are funny -- not amusing, but peculiar, adversarial, or not so nice. Your self-control can make or break you. Believe it or not, your looks and actions speak louder than your words. I know this is old-fashioned judging a book by its cover, but know this, the way you look helps you keep your secret.

> **"It's better to keep your mouth closed and let people think you're a fool, then to open your mouth and remove all doubt."**
> ~Abraham Lincoln

Ladies, believe it or not, your looks tell a lot about you; if your shallow, unstable, loose, great or small; whatever it is it's your secret. He should know you by the way you carry yourself, not by the way you dress. So, keep your mouth closed about your secrets and your legs too, ... Victoria has a secret so should you. Can you believe by looking at someone you can get all of that out of a look? True or false, yes, we do! *Question of the day* - Tell me how many times have you been wrong, judging peoples in the way they carry themselves? ... *(come on, I can't hear you).*

People's mannerisms tell a lot about them, not to the point of right and wrong, but to the point of suspicion.

Look at it like this, when you're trying to close a business deal, you show up fresh pressed like a million bucks; showing confidence and that speaks volume to your secret to what you're all about. See your secret is your secret sauce to seal the deals in life. Ladies your secret has power unknown, so before you let the cat out of the bag make sure you got it under control. *You know the cat! Smile...* This secret place is God's divine protection for you and your future. I'm not saying you can't have fun; I'm saying your fun needs to be with your *(soulmate, not cellmate),* because God has a plan for you.

Jeremiah 29:11 (ESV)
For I know the plans I have for you, declares
the Lord, plans for welfare and not for evil, to
give you a future and a hope.

One of the things I think God wants to do for us is restore everything that was stolen from us from material things all the way down to relationships. God is determined to bless us, so some of God blessings for us is a secret, hidden for us not from us. This is the "mystery" of the secret it has blessings connected to it, so you must know when to share your secret, and when to do the *Kenny rogers,* (know when) ... When God ends a conversation it's because He knows the end and don't want the enemy to stop the blessing. So, God says things like, *"we'll understand it better by-and-by."* ...it's His secret to and for us, He knows how to keep a secret and so should you. There's a secret I believe the world is waiting for, a secret like never before, and that's the secret time of Jesus return. We know He's coming back again, but when is the secret and it's a mystery. Now, do you see the power of secrets? We all have them. Jesus has the ultimate secret in terms of the day and time of his return, but there's a secret in the cosmos the air and in the sky that we all need help with and that's understanding this massive universe; the sun, moon and stars and all of space and everything in it... planets, galaxies... it's all a secret. Maybe not to you but space, water space, and sky space is a mystery to me. I have another secret to tell you about, the mystery of two people becoming one. Talk about a secret! This is the union of marriage. I think one of the penalties for not being a lady first is not knowing who and whose you are, or who you belong to. God thought so much of you that at the time of creation when He said, *"Let us make man,"* He made man and woman at the same time, but kept you, that's right you a secret inside of Adam until the coast was clear for you to come on the scene. Talk about a secret... when the universe thought creation was all over, God revealed you His ultimate secret; the ladies, the woman, that's you; God's ultimate plan for the earth to remain. Did you know, without you there's no me? This is one of the ways you know Adam and Eve was God's secret to reproduce life. Now that you know who's and who you are let's go back to the drawing board and get the record straight. Ladies, you are not an afterthought. You are and always was the key to open any door. That's why God called you the helpmeet; to help man meet all his obligations and fix this world we live in.

Now you know about Victoria's Secret and how she brought bloomers, to thongs and branded a piece of cloth and colonized people to live wearing clothing that covered half their buttock and made Billions. Ladies what's your secret you're not telling that will bring the world back to God? Remember the place God kept you hidden in Adam's side? That was to cover and protect you from harm, for such a time like this.

Genesis 2:22 (ESV)
"And the rib, which the Lord God
had taken from man, made he a woman,

It's your time to share the secret that only you know after all you are the helpmeet to mankind, so help a brother out and share your life saving secrets, not gossip or your personal information, *but lifesaving stuff.* You know everything about man because you lived inside of him once disguised as a Rib. Now I see why we love Ribs so much.... While Adam was exploring earth, naming the animals and such, the woman was doing the laundry an inside job. She was inside exploring man... so the next secret you share, let it be lifesaving. Victoria has a secret; so, should you.

When I think about Victoria I can't help but think about Jesus and Judas. (The betrayer of Jesus). The night He was betrayed, Jesus knew Judas would betray Him, but kept it a secret. Judas knew he was the betrayer, but said, "Lord is it I?" Oh yes, Jesus knew and understood just what was going on, but chose to keep it a secret, Jesus kept the secret for love's sake; Judas just lied.

Secret, secrets. Today, ladies, secret-keeping is not about lying; it's your prerogative, your right to choose what you share, when you share it, and with whom. Yes, it is your privilege to have your secret and use it to your advantage; to advance in life. Victoria had a secret and advanced in life, and so should you. The secret I think a lady should share today is to advance mankind by keeping the covenant of one woman for one man. Remember, it only takes a minute to fall in love, but a lifetime to build on that love. That's the secret to God's master plan for eternal life. So, instead of revealing the secrets of how big your *front or back* is, show your strength and let those secrets out, because the world not only wants to hear from you; we need the jewels you have. Victoria has a secret and so should you.

As I close this chapter I want to show you the power Woman possess, (A quality, ability, skill, etc....) The average man couldn't fundraise enough to save the babies and make the type of money woman make in the streets. I'm not glorifying sex trafficking I'm showing you the power you have, *good or bad.*

Can you believe these findings concerning **sex trafficking?** *The average age of entry into the sex trade is 14 years old.*

Last year sex traffickers made $100 Billion in profits. That's more than **(Intel, Microsoft, Google and Starbucks)** *combined.*

There are millions of trafficked sex slaves in the world today, up to 100,000 of whom live in the United States.

These numbers may have change since this book published; But one thing is clear, there is something special even great about women, and nothing can top her. There's one thing that's constant in our life's that everybody must do to live, we must eat and it doesn't make the money that sex traffic makes *(you don't have to have sex to live).* But for some reason it makes more than a necessity (food, water, shelter). Again, I'm not glorifying the sex trade! But keep in mind, Victoria has a Billion-dollar secret and so should you!

Chapter 6

You Don't Have the Right's to Have Sex

Genesis 1:28 (ESV)
And God blessed them. And God said to
them, "Be fruitful and multiply and fill the
earth and subdue it,

Genesis 9:1 (ESV)
And God blessed Noah and his sons and said
to them, "Be fruitful and multiply and
fill the earth.

Now this chapter is going to open your eyes like never before, because most of us did or we're doing it: thinking about and using sex just for pleasure filling the earth, we have part of it right but there's more to it than just doing the nasty! Smile… Don't get me wrong; sex is a pleasure getter, and it is smoking good, especially with your soulmate. But there is more to sex than pleasure. The pleasure has a *(blessing and a curse)* connected to it. Sex was initially made for married couples to build families and to establish God's Earthly Kingdom. In fact, the strongest union on earth is family. They're bigger and mean more to God than *(IBM and all the fortune 500 companies of this world)*. Now, I want to give full Disclosure: like Saul, before he became Paul, I was a total sinner. I was one of the biggest offenders of this text, but that doesn't stop it from being the truth. For most people, sex is the ultimate high. Using – abusing -- drugs and alcohol, nightclubbing, picking up one-night stands, and all white-collar crimes is absolutely sinning, but they have nothing on solicit sex. It's the greatest and most extreme pleasure on earth, truly feeling the pulse or inside of someone else's body is like the thrill of a life time. Think about the fastest scariest roller coaster or thrill ride you ever been on, compared to sex it just a walk in the park eating your favorite ice cream, know compares. I believe, if God made anything better on this earth for man then a woman *(He took it back to heaven with him). Can I get an amen? Amen, and amen again.*

I confess I was one of the biggest offenders in this area again, just so you don't think I am judging you. The lengths we go to for sex are beyond me. People do some of the craziest stuff for sex. For example, our prisons are full of sex offenders, because people steal sex like they are stealing cars or other material things; and the blessing is not on their actions. Some people do time in jail and some in hell, for stealing sex. Then there's us. We walk around living our not blessed sex life out on earth, but God gave sex to the union of man and woman in matrimony for free, with a purpose in mind. First to fill the *earth, subdue* it then have *dominion* over the whole earth. Look at the sequence God put it in. First, were not to rule over each other, but the things on the earth. Subdue it means to get things under control. We can talk about that for the next four years, or until we get a real president....

Most people don't know what subdue means, some of us think we are to screw everything walking, like you know who... *Mr.-Grab-Woman-Private-Parts.* Now remember my disclosure, that was not what our God meant when He said be fruitful and multiply. (Genesis 1:28) If you read the whole verse, it said, *And God blessed them...* the union of marriage. Don't look at me funny, I like getting my freak on too, because right now I can feel you looking at me like I'm crazy... like I didn't say I was one of the biggest offenders at one time. Just because I was doesn't give me or you the right to have sex outside of the union. That's all I'm saying, God established the union for a reason. It was for us to reunite and build families, not Gangs. If you want to see what a misguided missile looks like, keep having kids with sex demons, and no father *(fathers and dads are two different things)* or family structure. As powerful as a missile is, when it hits its right location, it kills everything in its path. It also has the same power when it hits the wrong location; hurting or killing everything in its path. If you knew the spirits that where transferred from sex it will blow your mind, wondering why you can't sleep at night, undecided in your thoughts it's because the spirit you just let in your body through sex, don't know you and wants to control you, so you're always fighting or upset with the other Spirit inside of you.

Sex is one of the ways of making weapons of mass destruction. Think about all the sex offenders and killers in this world. Where do you think they come from? Imagine, Hitler as a baby. Okay Stop... *"misguided missile"*. People, the devil tricks us. Think about the old school tendency toward having 10-15 kids. Who do you know that can raise that many kids and point them all in the right direction? (few far, and in between) Some of us got tricked, or could it be that the birth control we take for granted today was not readily available? Either way the *(baby boomers and millennials)* don't have to fall into the same trap, you can only give so much without losing yourself. Trust me my mother had nine plus, and we caught hell never enough of nothing, food, clothes or time, we had good times being poor not knowing it, but today knowing what my mother went through with all of us, she had to be delusional. I love you Mom, but some of the story's she told me about some of us coming here (being born), I'll never forget. I know it's a hard place, but please let me help you. Sex is dangerous outside of the union; do you know how many mothers die from child birth every day? outside of the union just complicate things even more.

Think of it as like riding in a fast car with no seatbelt. It's fun to drive along with the top down, your hair blowing in the wind, while you are going up and down hills at 80 mph. It's fun until you hit something – in this case, something that's not your union, you better have good insurance. Just so you don't think it's me talking, let's just look at the word of God, and see what He gave us permission to do, and not to do; and what He's blessings to have sex or *(Who he has ordained, to have the right to have sex?)* Please don't forget, *I'm just the mailman!*

God, not me, He put subdue right in the middle of filling the earth. Why? Because he knew things would get out of control with this sex thing, and it did. He said subdued first. God gave us permission, the rights or abilities to do something, that was given by someone who has the power to decide if it will be allowed or permitted. Sex is a beautiful thing. Sex has such a strong emotional tie to it that God said subdue first which means to get *Under Control.* Sex had messed a lot of people up today, so how do you call it love? Let's keep it real, most of us that are grown now from the 60s, and 70s, had some of the worst regret from having sex with people that were not right for us. Tell the truth and stop me *if I'm lying.* I knew a girl in high school who I wish I'd never said hi to, let alone sleep with. What a nightmare. A friend said to me, "TJ, you don't know those people leave that girl alone." Boy, I wish I had listened. It still haunts me today, and it happened in my 20s. I'm 55 now, doing the speed limit, living right, and still getting tickets from that summer fling of sex outside the blessing. I'm still having regrets, so watch who you decide to *"be fruitful and multiply with";* it could be a trap. Even marriages could be a set up, so make sure you are equally yoked. This sex thing is huge. Don't you wish this book was out before you said *"I do, I did, or I will"* before you had sex with him or her? Lmbo…I'm only laughing to keep from crying, like Sarah and Abraham when Sarah loan her husband Abraham to her mad servant, what a big mess that was, the servant got pregnant and almost cost them everything. Me too. *(read Genesis 16).*

I once heard an elder gentleman, call kissing, *"Up town shopping for downtown business" Boy*, aren't some of us getting the business right now from sex? For some of us it was like the kiss of death; it caused us to be with people who had nothing -- absolutely nothing -- to do with our destiny on this earth. If you could turn back the hands of time, what would you do??? Don't ask me! People just don't know how evil sex is outside of the union of marriage. Like I said, it's the ultimate pleasure, but you must consider all those involved when you have sex: the ones you're having it with, and the ones who may come from the act. You must consider even the person's place in life and that person's mental and emotional state of mind, *(please don't overlook mental & emotional state)* so that you don't end up screwing a killer, or worst a stalker. How could the stalker be worst then the killer? I'm glad you asked. The killer stops ones the job is done, but a stalker is like the *Energizer Bunny,* just keep going… I bet you never thought of that. Entering someone else's body, or allowing someone to enter your body, is huge. How do you say you love someone one day, and the next day beat the Hell out of that same person? Talk shows are making millions from the repercussions people endure after having sex with busters. Producers of shows like *The Jerry Springer Show, Maury, Real Housewives of Atlanta, Wendy Williams, and Love and Hip-Hop* are having a laugh on folks having sex outside the blessing. It's big business. They call the consequences and repercussions entertainment, I call it evil. *How's that working for you?* Other people making millions off your booty call. Now you tell me if you have the right to have sex?

When our forefathers were stolen from the Motherland Africa, the entire enterprise was Evil. Families were divided from one another; kids were with their parents one day, and then the next day they were taken, to never see their parents again. Their Heritage, their country, their traditions achievements, and beliefs... all stolen! That was part of their history, which is everything in a person's life. That's what people live for: their heritage. People spend millions trying to find their heritage on websites like *Ancestry.com.* That's how huge it is! To take away a people's history and their way of doing things... I have a tear in my eyes now thinking about it. Now they want to charge you to find what they stole! I told you that sex was evil, but steeling people for their homeland is still at the top.

Read one of Mark Twain's Quotes:

When the rich rob the poor, it's called business. When the poor fight back it's called violence.

Everybody has a home to go visit, except African Americans. Think about it, that must be the highest level of evil ever. Even the Holocaust, during which millions of Jews and others were killed, millions of Jews, during our World Wars dwarf losing *Everything.* Losing your way of living, culture, and land forever is almost as bad as going to visit Hell for vacation! That's evil! *Real talk...* It breaks my heart. I mentioned these two atrocities to show you how evil has ruined lives and histories.

Now, let's look what sex does to innocent children every day when there's no mother and father in the home. Sometimes, kids come home to one or no family member. Baby daddy is like living with a stranger, he's like *(Houdini the magic man),* now you see him, now you don't. A person who has pleasure sex outside of the blessing is setting him - or - herself up for trouble.

Sex outside of the union of marriage does the same thing slaver did to us, can you believe that! What was a key strategy that slave owners used beyond the cruelty, beatings, and free labor? It was separating families. Family separation is what happens every day when sex is misused. The keyword is *"blessing"* just like the days of old. Kids today are still lost and ripped away from all our traditions and history in the name of love, or should I say sex. Why? because you don't have the right to have sex unmarried. ***Point blank.*** God's ultimate plan for sex was family. I want to do the nasty too, because it's God's ultimate pleasure on earth. So, I understand how you feel, but we must do it God's way. Sometimes I wish there was another way around it, but it's God's way or the highway to (hell).

Of course, people who are married with families break up as well. That's true; but God still blessed their union. The split is just another law that was broken, like sex before marriage, because what God put together no one is supposed to separate.

Mark 10:9 (ESV)
***What therefore God has joined together,
let not man separate."***

As I got older, when I saw families together, it would break my heart; not because they were a family, because we're all supposed to have them. It broke my heart because *(a child without a father is like an explorer without a compass).* In too many cases, that child doesn't have his or her father around because the parents just had to have sex outside the union. Every kid has a mother and father, but not in the home.

Sometimes, kids look at me with my family like, *"Who is he?"* like where did he come from? I don't know my older kids who were born when I was unmarried. It's sad; because of what I was influence with cause me not to get to know them at that time, and now getting to know them it breaks my heart because their all Great kids, they don't know me, and I don't know them either. It's getting better now. They are my kids, yes, but we are not family. Trust me, family is everything. So, stop screwing around and subdue your nature. Get it under control and build your family, which should be everything you strive for.

We can go on and on about sex humiliating and annihilating people's lives every day. Not only are kids lost, but families are lost also. Have you ever gone to a family reunion gathering and found out that the guys or girls you were hitting on is your cousin... **that's Bessy Mae daughter, on your cousin side twice removed...** yeah, I know you have, because it's happened to me? Families are lost when we do things our way outside of the union. We don't know who's who. We take it lightly, but *sin sucks the life out of you...* all sin. Everyday women are deceived by the ones who are supposed to cover them... Men. How in God's green earth are we going to make it in this life if the ones that are supposed to help you keep hurting you? Life and God's history, and the way of doing things is largely a story of how men and women was supposed to rule over this earth together, supporting and loving one another in the union of marriage. I can't tell you just what happened, but somehow, we got it twisted and the Order God gave us just went out the window. It's so bad now that we don't know who to hug and kiss no more. What happen? *(This union is huge)* ... We were supposed to be fruitful and multiply in the union of marriage. Anything outside of the union, as far as sex is concerned, in God's eye, is a curse, (sin) *(In God's eyes)* but we still do it. And forget about same sex in God eyes.

I saw two people together of the same sex one day, and they were shy about being together in public. Knowing something was wrong in their spirit. Remember I said sex was evil outside the union? that was the spirit that made them feel shy, our spirit man knows right from wrong, we just be tripping. Have you ever got ready to do something wrong, and something on the inside of you alerts you with a warning? That's the spirit man! *The real you.* They knew it, so they hid from normal people, if there's such a people. Just like Adam and Eve hid from God in the garden, when they knew something was wrong that they did. People know, but the devil got a hold on them. *I bind him right now in the name of JESUS!* Satan let them go right Now.

Don't chop my head off, it's God's order to fulfill the earth. Most relationships outside of the marriage must be the most stressful thing going. Been there done that! Marriage has them also, but the blessing is connected to them. We have reality shows of all kinds, making mad money off this type of life style. *"Housewives from Two-below The Dark side of Nowhere,"* TV reality shows talking about people's problems all day and night. Mainly because they're not bless, and they know it's a market of wrong doing, and a Money Maker. Who does that? I'm not saying all of it is bad, and I'm not saying you can't date, but most relationships are not dating. They are setting up shop, playing house, with kids and house bills, living together. Some women are doing everything wifey does, with none of the benefits sleeping around and doing things right in the front of the kids. Now the children think this is the way to do relationships, it's a shame, and we wonder why they're fighting all the time, it's because they're not blessed... wait not the people... *but the fake union.* I did it, and it took all the fun out of my future bride to be, so I got it right. Ladies if you want to be wifey one day, or the one and only, please get another plan. If you want the truth keep reading. If you don't want the truth keep reading... because I've got some good information for Ya.

In relation to the era before certain social revolutionary inventions such as the automobile, we had the *(horse and buggy)* because that was the way people got around. During the old days, Dad would hook up and unhook the horse from the buggy, because you don't carry the buggy around with you all day. Sometimes you just ride the horse by itself, but when you want to travel and carry stuff across town, you put the horse in front of the buggy to carry family, people, and things around. That makes sense to get around town with your belongings. Most people today shacking up, have the buggy in the front of the horse; going nowhere. Everybody knows that not how you enjoy the ride in a buggy. The kids see this type of lifestyle and think that's the way to date and live. Some repeat the cycle, just to end up hurt, dating, and fighting; just to find out that's not the way to build families. When you start giving out free anything, like milk and cookies, people let me tell you something it's hard to stop, because milk and cookies are good anytime. Now you want to sell your stuff after giving it for free. Trust me on this, that's not how you get to the finish line in relationships and definitely not for marriage. I don't think so! When I say sell, I mean now you want to get serious in a relationship with the person that has been getting *(friend benefits)* ... He's buying, just not from you, because you are, or were, a freebie. When you decide to change, settle down, and start a family, but you already have three or four kids outside of the marriage, the transition can be a nightmare -- not the kids, but the baby mama, daddy drama. I know what I'm saying is hard, but the truth will set you free. When a guy gets your cookies for free, your value on the relationship stock market just bottoms out. So, the question should be to men, why do we bag so dame much if we know that we're not moving forward with that person? *(That's the million-dollar question.)*

If you feel like you must have sex and can't wait for your husband, or wife if you can, when you come to a new relationship, come like **Macaulay Culkin,** Alone (no baggage). Because it will rob you before you get started with your new boo.

The only sin I know with no repentance is blasphemy against the Holy Spirit. With that said, repent, get up, and like Jesus told the adulterous woman, *go and sin no more.* If the bags you're bringing to this new relationship don't have groceries in them, it's going to be a hard sell. And if by chance the relationship works the kids need to know what to call him, if they call him uncle, and he's sleeping in your mother bed, call the police; he's an impostor... (A person who deceives other by pretending to be someone else). Ladies make him make you an honest woman. As you see there's a lot in preparing for true love.

"Buying" is used as a metaphor for marriage, and if he is only having fun with you for free, he's only having fun and not planning to invest in a relationship with you. Now do you see why there's a penalty for not being a lady first? Lead on's are great for networking but in physical relationships it's devastating to your success. Now tell yourself two times: *"put the buggy behind the horse, so we can move forward."* That is, if you want to go somewhere in life and enjoy the view. You may have even been living with this person without marriage, but that was then, this is now, so change your way of doing things, and let's get up the street in life building families.

Today, I work as a cosmetologist. We have rules and laws pertaining to hair and chemicals. When you are applying a relaxer to a customer's hair, you can never use one chemical on top of another chemical. For instance, when a customer is getting a relaxer, the stylist can never use permanent color at the same time the relaxer is applied without threatening the integrity of the hair. That's a rule. On the other hand, the stylist can try to apply those two chemicals and hope nothing goes wrong. If a stylist does that, he or she has now broken very important hair laws. Taking that kind of chance is almost like running a yellow light. You might make it through or you might not; but in both cases, the rules caution you, just like God's word. Laws penalize you, and that's just what premarital sex and shaking gives you, rules and the laws. One cautions you and the other penalizes you. You can have premarital sex; the caution is the kids. Don't run when they get here. The penalties are child support; pay it. The kids are a blessing from God, so watch who you make them with. Sex is fun in the beginning, but watch out, because you really don't have the right to have sex outside the marital union. So, much can go wrong.

When I was growing up some men, (OG's) would think the more women you had made you a man. *FYI... that's a lie from the pits of hell.* That doesn't make you a man. If that was the case, animals, rodents, roaches, and dogs would be men. Obeying God's word first is what makes you a man. Next, loving the one woman you have. That's what an OG's (older gentleman) should be telling the young men. Anybody can screw around, but if you commit to loving that one-woman God gave you, then you can call yourself a man. And If he takes care of his family, wife, and kids, he's like a *Superhero.* Most men brains are tainted with booty meat, especially if their fathers were unsaved or misguided.

When you buy a car, if you have any trouble with it, the first thing you look for in the car is the owner's manual to find out how to fix it. Well, the same goes for relationships. God made you both, so why not go back to the manual. The B-I-B-L-E, *God's, Basic, Instruction, Before, Leaving, Earth* to see how to manage the relationship? We all know if you're not accountable to someone, you have no one to answer to. That's why I said if he's not saved, that type of person will screw a rock. We must get back to the old landmark; God's way of doing things. Not having the rights to have sex doesn't mean you can't have sex, it just means we must do it God's way for his Blessing. As I'm writing I can hear you saying what about all the famous and wealthy people that have unmarried sex. Yes, they are famous and wealthy, but

God's blessings are far greater than the world's wealth. Gaining the world and losing your soul is an uneven or bad deal. Yes, *(Hollyweird)* make it look good, but divorce is not God's way. Every day some actor or actress is in the arms of another person from the big screen making fake love for the movies. It can create jealousy and strife in the home life of married actors. Gaining wealth at the expense of losing your family and putting yourself in an uncompromising place It is not the best deal for your family or your eternal existing. I'm not saying it's like that for everyone, but it's rampant. The money is great, don't get me wrong, I get it, but you can't afford to be on the wrong side of eternity, if there is such a place. The thing about it is, if there's no place where all good!... BUT if there is your *grass, will get cut.*

Here's my point, you can ask the time teller how much time you have left in eternity, heaven or hell, because you know we're built to last. You're going to live eternity *"somewhere"...heaven or hell.* The time teller will say to you after a thousand years have passed that time hasn't even started yet. Trust me, you don't have the right to have sex and end up on the wrong side of eternity, in the age to come. Stop letting people tell you they don't see nothing wrong with a little bump and grind. Ask R. Kelly how that's working for him today! That's true with your spouse, it's even a great song, me and my wife like to play it when were…Smile, but outside of the marriage union, with a man and a woman it is more dangerous than drinking strychnine. In fact, it's just like strychnine, it is a little poisonous substance that can be used in very small amounts in medicine to heal your sickness; a bad thing made good. Sex on the other hand in small amounts condemn your soul to hell. *Your flesh will send you to hell and won't show up.* That's why I said sex is like strychnine, it's a good thing within God's blessing, outside of the union of God, it's poison.

Remember the song **Poison?** Bell, Biv, Devoe, former members of Boyz *to* Men, said *"never trust a big butt and a smile…* it's **poison."** That's why I said you don't have the right to have sex. If you take strychnine by itself it will kill you, though strychnine in small amounts is actually safer than sex outside of marriage in small amounts. Sex just puts you in the wrong place with God and man. I'm not telling you to go drink strychnine. I'm saying that if you're trying to make it into the kingdom of God, you don't have the right to have sex outside of the union of marriage. *Remember: rules caution you. Laws when broken, penalize you.*

Romans 6:23 (ESV)
For the wages of sin is death, but the gift of
God is eternal life in Christ Jesus our Lord

This verse gives us the intelligence that the wages of sin is death. Death in God is not the same as dying in sin. There's an eternal gift in Jesus Christ. Therefore, you can't afford to have sex in the scheme of eternal life. It's just too *doggone long!* I don't want to bring doom and gloom to your life's pleasures. My goal is to bring quality and understanding to the power that lives within you. You are **woman:** God's masterpiece. You are not on this earth to just have sex and make babies. You were placed here to lead, rule and have dominion, not to be used and abused by every ding-a-ling you meet. You are here as

God's finest creations, there nothing you can't do when you put your mind to it, remember you are the helpmeet that can help mankind meet all of its obligations. Case in point, there's a woman in the Bible called the adulterous woman. I know you've heard of her. She's recorded in John 8:3-4.

John 8:3-4 (ESV)
The scribes and the Pharisees brought a
woman who had been caught in adultery
and placing her in the midst they said to him,
"Teacher, this woman has been caught in the
act of adultery.

This is a very interesting story, because the word of God says this woman was caught in adultery. Now, it only addresses this woman. That's the interesting part, because she was caught, but with who? *Any who.* Jesus was there and save her life because it was customary to stone relationships outside of their marriage in those days. Today we just sleep with whatever, and whoever, if the custom were the same today as then bodies would be dead everywhere, all down main street. I think the part I want to bring out is, was this woman having sex by herself? No. It was at the same time Jesus was teaching about the (Feast of Tabernacles) had just concluded the day before. Many visitors were still in town attracted by the appearance of the *rabbi, "Jesus Christ"*...but the Rude and disruptive Pharisees were bent on confronting Jesus; abruptly bringing the adulterous woman into the midst of his teaching. Jesus stopped his teaching to teach and defend his masterpiece; the woman. Stoning this woman was certain had Jesus not been there. It is still unclear why the authorities wanted to stone just the woman, after all she was caught, but not the man. How? *(This is a mystery to me! How was she caught, but not him)?* Could it be you don't have the right to have sex outside of the blessed union? ...or is the woman's body more superior than the man's concerning the weaker vessel? Ladies see how uneven the sex game is, the men that just screwed you is now trying to kill you, trust me you don't have the rights to have sex.

One thing is sure, death was associated with sex. Could it had just been that the religious leaders were trying to trap Jesus into doing or saying something that was contrary to the law. If He would have said stone her, He would have contradicted Jewish laws. If He would have said don't stone her, He would have discounted Rome laws, which does not permit Jews to carry out their own execution. Remember rules caution you, laws penalize you. Jesus, came to seek and save, so He politely said to the woman, *"sin no more"* ...implying that sex outside of marriage is a sin that can kill you, or in the worst case, sin will send your soul to hell, and won't show up! Yes, Jesus has us covered by His blood, but He also has laws. Sin no more! implies Jesus forgave her, He did not condemn her, neither did He condone her sin. FYI, *sin sucks the life out of you.*

Jesus came that we might have life, so choose life, isn't it interesting that God gave us sex with stipulations. Agreement was given to the union of marriage. When it's done right with a man and a woman, it's not sex anymore, it's God's way to replenish the earth and to keep families together and strong, God called it to be *fruitful and multiply.* So, He said be fruitful (to produce a good result), not to be sexually loose with people *(In my own words)* *"producing a lot of sex with your spouse is a good thing".* Therefore, you must know your rights. Can you imagine having car insurance, but then getting into an accident and not knowing you're covered so that you can make a claim? That's what sex outside of the union of marriage is like. What a waste. You're not covered for two reasons: one, you don't know what your rights are, as your coverage is listed in your policy (God's word). So, you're penalized. Reason number two: you're breaking God's laws. Now can you see why sex is overrated, valued, and highly praised in the wrong ways? Without a doubt, sex must be the highest pleasure on earth, but you will never know the true pleasure sex brings until you do it God's way and read your policy, the Bible. As you're reading I can hear you saying, who do he think he is trying to tell me my rights? I'm glad you ask. Someone that made hundreds of mistakes and know where all the pitfalls of life are located, so you don't have to fall in them!

One day my wife's car was having problems, so we just took it to a local mechanic, who tried to figure out the problem, to no avail. We took it back to the original manufacturer, they looked at the car and knew within minutes what the problem was with the car. If we had done that the first time, we would have saved time, money and heartache. Well, that's my point with sex, if you don't want the headaches and problems it brings, take it back to the manufacture and do it God's way. He has already given the man permission to find you. It will save you time, money, heartaches, and yes... your soul. Believe me, I know.

Remember my earlier disclosure, I was the chief sinner, been there done that, got the t-shirt. I know what I'm talking about, your true spouse fits you in a way you cannot even imagine, like socks on feet or hands in a glove. You guys will go places in each other you never knew you had when he finds you, *"can you see him coming now"?*

True story...

What I'm about to say is grown folk stuff, So, kids put the book down or close your eyes for a second. Gentlemen if you ever want your penis to take a long walk in the park of your woman's vagina and stretch out, find your soulmate and little peter will go down some roads he never knew was there and vice-ver-sa. Trust me on this one, there are pockets on your woman that you never explored Yet. I might have to ask my mother in love to put the book down for a moment also, smile... Me and my wife pray cried and made love all at the same time one day, I never been down what road before, until I did it God's way. It happened to me.

What I discovered in a healthy heterosexual relationship, is love and sex are two different things. Therefore, some people I know don't know love or never fall in love, they never had it, they had sex. Anybody can have that. Making love is reserved for God's blessing. Boy and Girlfriends are just that, *(friends);* but your wife, spouse, soulmate takes you to another level in the art of making love. He or she supports and challenges you to be great every day. Have you ever used generic brands to cook food, it's good, but there's nothing like the *real thing baby...* enough said? There are so many broken people trying to figure out what's wrong with them.

"News flash" there's nothing wrong with you, because God don't make no junk. Ones your man figure out your value it's on and cracking, this is especially true for women because you're the vehicle to life. When you're with a man or different men, the stuff he leaves behind in you after sex can kill a herd of pigs. The thing about sex is it's great, but for God's purpose; we misuse it in so many ways. All throughout the word of God, sex was frowned upon outside of the marriage. Before I go too far, go with me to the word of God and let's see how evil sin and demons are.

Matthew 8:31 (ESV)
"And the demons begged him, saying,
"If you cast us out, send us away into
the herd of pigs."

We learned a few things in this passage about sin that's associated with hurting or killing things in its way. We see that demons recognize the deity of Christ. Next, they're limited in their knowledge, but they will be judged by Christ.

In verse 29, the first thing the demon said to Jesus is, *"What have we to do with you?"* This is a powerful revelation! (will explain later in book). They knew Jesus' power and still wanted to kill the herd of swine; no regard for life. That's just what sexual sin does. It won't stop until it kills. It will use anyone or anything in its path. It only has one job and it's to separate you from God and eternal life. Sin is so evil and selfish that it will kill whatever, kids, dog, cat, pig whatever allowed it to come in.

We use phrases to justify are sinful lifestyles; like us today saying thing like *"I don't see nothing wrong with a little bump and grind".* That sounds cute, trust me there's a lot wrong with a little or a lot of grinding outside of marriage. Hell is not going to be a party. I think the point I want to bring out in this chapter is, if man is the head, the woman would have to be the crown. We must start treating them that way. Most people put their hat on the top shelf when they take it off, so it doesn't get crash or set on. Well, that's just what we need to do with our women; put them on the top shelf of our life and stop pimping our help meets, (woman)…outside of the union of marriage, because it dishonors our woman and God. If you really love your woman, make her an honest woman.

1 Thessalonians 4:3 (ESV)
For this is the will of God, your sanctification:
that you abstain from sexual immorality

I hate to rain on your parade, because we can go on and on… with this topic on who's right and who's wrong. Well, we're both wrong, the only one that's right concerning who and when to have sex with is God. Sexual immorality of all kinds is sinful… *lust, adultery, fornication, incest, homosexuality, and bestiality (sex with animals).*

In short sex within marriage is used as a good thing; a gift from God to be enjoyed and celebrated by both husband and wife, not singles. Please my brothers and sisters, I don't make the rules and I don't want to be a party pooper, but sin Sucks. It's killed too many of my friends, before I came to know Christ. Now that I know, if you're in Christ we will see each other again in heaven, if you die before I get to see you, but if you die in sin we'll never cross paths again; at least that's My eternal goal. So, let's have good clean fun so we can live again. *That was an altar call.* We must get this one right. Let me leave you with Proverbs 5:1.

Proverbs 5:1 (ESV)
My son, be attentive to my wisdom;
incline your ear to my understanding

I think the thing most people don't understand is every time you sleep or have sex with a person that's not your spouse you just slept with everyone they slept with in one date. Remember, that's the same demon that killed the pigs that are now trying to kill you, because it's sin, all kinds of demons are connected to it trying to suck the life out of you. So when your Boo is charming you, it's cute I know, but he's actually trying to kill you, not with a knife or gun, but with sex. I know that deep, but it's the truth. *Sin sucks the life out of you.*

The thing God left on this earth to get us from earth to glory is the Bible, God's basic instructions before leaving earth, and we must try to follow it to the letter, because man is coming up short on living a clean life. Just look at the past failures pertaining to sex outside of the union of marriage. Nobody wants to talk about it but look at the lives wasted. Our jails are filled with kids, men and women. Every day we face broken homes one way or another, kids are fatherless, mothers are husbandless and raising kids by themselves. Gangs are rampant. All of that comes from illicit sex. Not knowing where your parents are is not cool. Too many children bear this burden because of sex outside the union, which is not permitted by God. I know it happens both way with marriages as well as singles. The wrath is death physical and spiritual because that kind of sex outside of the union is not blessed. Look what's happening to the kids who are the product of sex outside the blessed union of marriage. Please Note: this is not every situation but #1 is enough. Take a close look at Genesis 1:28.

If your trying to find your way in the things of God and life, concerning your life choices, these few scriptures will help you get from earth to glory. This is mainly for people struggling with their identity, this will help, it's God's medicine.

Genesis 1:28 (ESV)
And God blessed them. And God said to them, "Be fruitful and multiply and fill the earth and subdue it, and have dominion

Genesis 9:1 (ESV)
And God blessed Noah and his sons and said to them, "Be fruitful and multiply and fill the earth.

Leviticus 18:22 (KJV)
Thou shalt not lie with mankind, as with womankind: it is abomination.

If you believe God created man and woman in His image, then God blessed them, and commanded them to be fruitful, multiply, and fill the earth, then any other way is not God's way. Any other way is not associated with his blessings according to the scriptures. This is my cry to women because it's always mama's baby and daddy's maybe. Women lose all hope and sense of direction after the baby is here, when the fathers are gone, nowhere present, nowhere to be found. Now the woman is empty, trying to figure out what happened to the man she loved and who she thought loved her. That's why I said those two words, *(love and sex)*, are too close for comfort and misleading. After all, she gave him everything: all of herself everything he wanted; all the bells and whistles the *(famous Combo)*, please tell me you know what the combo is? And he still left her.

What do you do when you did and gave your all? What do you do when your promise turns to a problem? The hopelessness some women face today is the result of empty promises from the men they felt they were supposed to trust and help. But how do you help someone who constantly lets you down or fails you? This is all happening in the name of love and sex. *"I love you."* We say it too easily connected with sex before marriage. What we're really saying is, *"Can we have unblessed sex?"* Maybe the better answer to that question would be, **"if this is love, can you love me less?"**

Therefore, I say you don't have the right to have sex. In my opinion love and sex are overrated concerning relationships, because the two are tied so closely together during the act; but are actually very different in the support they give one another. A man may think, when a woman is making noises during intercourse and climax, that he has hit a home run. Well, he did in some regards, but that's just getting up to bat. Now it's time to run the bases. When a child comes into the world, the first people he or she should see are *mommy* **and** *daddy*.

Parents being present is <u>first base.</u> My wife and son are my responsibility that I accepted from God. Parents **taking ownership** of their responsibilities is <u>second base...</u> That's what we need more of, men who accept their responsibilities -- not just to have sex, but to give the woman you're screwing your name, take it to the next level and run all the bases. You know, love her and lead her. Then have all the nasty, funky, sex you can after that. I once heard a man say that *"a woman's womb is a womb that can't be healed: the more you hit it, the better it feels"*.

Can you tell I grow up a fresh little boy, Lmbo...? So, gentlemen, accept your responsibilities, put a ring on it, and get to hitting Home runs, RBIs *(Runs batted in)* and Grand slams. Then you have the right to have sex with your spouse; one man and one woman. Any other way is not God's way.

For too long, women have been carrying men. I think it's time for the men to re-turn the favor, and not just carry her, but cover her as well. That's <u>third base.</u> She's not just your spouse, she's precious, rare, and very valuable. She brings you great wealth, and she carries a high price. If you read your Bible, you'll find she carries your favor in this life. That's high praise, and most men don't know the woman he eats and sleeps with every day houses the highest expression from God in her: It called *favor.* Every day he goes to work trying to get the boss to like him or show him favor. The only thing he has to do is find a wife and treat her right and the favor of God will be all over him; just like that. That's how valuable women are to men. The favor in a woman is God's way of assuring success in the union of marriage, so our women won't be left behind. His masterpiece, the woman, keeps families together and show the family how to honor and respect one another. If we knew the history of woman and what she came through from the days of old, just like **(Harriet Tubman), was an American abolitionist and political activist. Born into slavery, Tubman escaped and subsequently made some thirteen missions to rescue approximately seventy enslaved people, family and friends.** And the list goes on and on... After all she (woman) only carried our Lord and Savior, now she is carrying (mankind) her children to freedom, talk about amazing she is to be celebrated, never just tolerated. She has made a great impact in everyday life and in the spiritual realm. Isn't it good to know women were made for man and she once lived in man, and man came through woman? who's was first? That's how valuable we are to each other. Read your Bible. We came first, both of us, which means we are inseparable. It's like the chicken and the egg: both have great value.

Women are to be held in high esteem, in and out of the Bible. For example, Hannah single-handedly purified, revived, and revitalized the religious life of the entire Jewish nation. Mary, the mother of our Lord and Savior, will forever be referenced as the most blessed among women, because she believed that God would perform the miraculous. In the scriptures, women were more conspicuous than men in religious devotion. When Jesus entered his ministry, women intuitively responded to his teaching, sympathized with him in his darkest hours, and found in him their benefactor and friend.

When Jesus was dying on the cross, it was women who were the last to leave the cross, women who were the first ones at the tomb on the resurrection day, and women who were the first to proclaim the glorious news of His victory over the grave. *(Don't ever forget that!).*

This is the power women have. Their faith and prayers were mingled with those of the apostles in preparation for Pentecost all throughout the Christian era. Men and the church owed women more than they realized for the prayers, loyalty, and gifts of the female members of the early church. Today, churches all over the world would go to pieces if it were not for the presence, perseverance, and prayers of women. It was said, *"What is better than wisdom?"* Women. And, what is better than a good woman? *Nothing.* God said it's not good for man to be alone, so He made woman. So, ladies remember, sex is beneath you, that's why you don't have the rights to have sex. You are to be loved, respected, honored, and celebrated... *never just screwed...* and that's home plate men. She's far more than a one-night stand or a nut. She's wisdom dressed in favor. For more education on the power of woman, read Proverbs 18:22 and 1st peter 3:7 and learn what you been missing out on. It changed my life! That's right, she doesn't have the rights to have "sex," because she a love-making, child-having, vehicle-to-life creative, machine that birth class our Lord, Christ. Don't limit her to one thing ever again, she Mother earth, the life giver.

Chapter 7

If I Only Knew What He Wanted

The world we live in today is so uncertain about almost everything, from politics to identity fraud, and all in between. It's really hard to trust people on their word today. This is especially true for women, because while the man is supposed to be the one person who should be able to act as a fix-it-all protector for their women, their marriages, and their families from the Creator's viewpoint, many women cannot depend on their men to play that role.

Today, as it has always been, fraud is associated with tricking people, almost on every level. Fraud is an unfortunate part of the world we live in today. Anytime a person pretends to show that he or she is not what the Creator made him or her to be, while saying that the Creator intention was a mistake that person is committing a type of fraud or trickery mixed with confusion. That person is willing to commit fraud while using the name the Creator gave them, *(man or woman),* after all we're only talking about the one who made everything! and put the moon and stars and all the galaxies into space. So how in the H-E-DOUBLE-HOCKEY-STICKS can we come along centuries later and say *I'm supposed to be the opposite sex of what the Creator made me to be.* That's absurd; trickery at its highest level. How in this great world are we to know what's truth when today honesty and truth are such lonely words? Think about what God says in Jeremiah 1:5 about how long He knew us:

Jeremiah 1:5 (ESV)
"Before I formed you in the belly I knew you."

That's a long time. If God knew who you were going to be before you were formed, how can you say that our God make a mistake making you who you are?

Who and what do we believe? I recommend the word of God, because it's a guide for everything, both a tool and a how-to manual to repair and to keep things from breaking down in your life. Yes, it's the Bible; God's basic instructions before leaving earth. You know it's bad when people today don't even know which bathroom to crap in. People today, we have all kinds of ideas on how to live, I don't know if it's the *(boomers or the millennials ideas)*, but I can assure you there's only one way: God's way. We have people who have all kinds of degrees and don't have a clue about God's basic instructions before leaving earth. It's not the degrees that matter; it's God's Word that is the final say. Bringing the truth to people is not easy sometimes. But as an ordained Elder, I'm mandated to report abuse of any kind. I'm out on the front lines the (streets) reporting, hopefully helping my brothers and sisters, but mainly the sisters on the *Penalties for Not Being A Lady First.*

It's not the ladies' fault as much as the men who must shoulder most of the blame. We men have failed to hold up our end of the deal since the beginning of time; so, I'm here today writing it in **books, movies and plays** telling it like it is. I want to bring out one of the most insane things I've ever heard. My knees are knocking because it came from someone I believe in and I love his style and mannerisms, he's all over television game shows and everywhere, but this one thing I can't let go. Although I agree with a lot of his stuff, and I use some of his advice in my everyday life; but the 90 days rule before having sex was the last straw.

When I heard this very influential man make this claim, I knew I had a duty – a mandate from God -- to report that statement as a form of abuse. I couldn't find any reference to any 90-day rule in the Bible. The idea of sex after 90 days contradicts God's laws – that's why I couldn't find any reference to it in the Word. I am mandated to report abuse of all kind, and people – especially those whose words influence others -- who promote such an unlawful statement as a 90-day rule are being abusive. Women and (mankind) have been taking a beating by having sex outside of the blessing.

Genesis 1:28 (ESV)
And God blessed them. And God said to them, "Be fruitful and multiply and fill the earth and subdue it,

Ladies and gentlemen, the keyword here is, (Them). God never blessed sex; He blessed them through the union of marriage. Sex never had anything to do with a set time, say of 90 days; but it has everything to do with the blessings God bestows on man and woman in the marital union: marriage. God's time is the timeline for sex, Not 90 days. Ignoring God's timeline is one of the reasons women don't know what men really want. It sure isn't just sex! We all want sex. If that was all he wanted, he would stay with you after the act. Hello...

So, now we all know that what he wants *sho' ain't sex.* It's much more than that. Now we know sex doesn't mean he wants you; it means he wants to use you to release something. I said it earlier and it deserves to be *reiterated:* your degrees are great, but if what you have learned is not associated with God's basic instructions, we must correct. Women find out that after waiting 90 days to have sex, and he still moves on to someone else. The timing doesn't have anything to do with days or sex, but relationship; relating to God. The blessings of God come after marriage concerning sex. What part of this don't we understand? The sex before or after? Because the only ones losing out because of our confusion are the babies. This sex and drug thing destroyed lot of lives, the reason I but drugs in there is because it seems like they go together, like Ice cream and apple pie, so I heard. Smile...

Let me help you, plain and simple. Sex before marriage is a curse concerning God's word; and most of us did it. Sex before marriage is not blessed. I know in the world system it seems to work, but from a Christian standpoint, we are trying to live eternal life in heaven. Honoring God's blessing of sex within marriage doesn't apply to you if you're not interested in eternal life in heaven. Note: That I said heaven because we're going to live somewhere heaven or hell forever! The reason our electronic devices work is because they are connected to a source of their power. Until you get plugged into a true or right connection, you can forget about your device working, physically or spiritually.

In the same vein, you can have all the sex you want after one day or 90 days it won't work. The sex might be good, but God's blessing is far from it. Now don't get me wrong, sometimes my flesh wants what it wants also.... But, I have heaven in my view; so, to do something that blocks my view would mean I would have to suffer some penalties. Yes, we want sex, but the woman I want to spend my life with has to be more than arms, legs and a big butt for me. Remember that you can get sex anywhere, but a soulmate is hard to find.

When I was growing up, sex was all I wanted from girls. There were certain girls from the other side of town I would see from time to time. We liked each other in a casual way, and we would get together sometimes and make out, you know do the nasty. That would go on for years with no connection; we were just *"funning."* So, we thought we didn't know any better. That's another reason the 90-day rule won't work. Most men can play the we're-friends-we're-cool game for years with no commitment. Oh yeah, I've done it and so have most of you. Ninety days is just another way of playing the same game.

If you want to know the real deal, listen to some of the artists who said it best in their songs: Tina Turner's *"What's Love Got to Do with It?"* or Janet Jackson's *"What Have You Done for Me Lately?"* Think about the no-nonsense declaration in the late Gwen Guthrie's hit song *"Ain't Nothing Going on But the Rent: "No romance without finance.... You got to have a J-O-B if you wanna be with me....* And *"Single Ladies* (Put a Ring on It,"

Beyonce proclaims, "...if you liked then you should have put a ring on it." I'm not saying these declarations of independence will fix your sex life, but an attitude adjustment might help you find out what kind of man you're working with. Lots of men never want to make the commitment to one woman anyway, and all sex does is complicate things, especially if he's not the marrying kind.

I am sure you're wondering what that means. Oh, a man who is not the marrying kind is the one who gets what he wants without committing to a relationship or being connected to one woman. That kind of man never makes an investment in you or in any lasting relationship. In the past, some may have called him a *"good-time Charlie,"* which means he only wants to have fun.

When a woman gives a man sex before marriage, chances are she has one idea and he have another. She may be seeing a future long-term relationship, while he may have already checked out of the interaction with her. Sex means one thing to men and another thing to women. The woman is dreaming of her future house, kids, and white picket fence around her property with her future husband – the man she just had sex with -- you know; the American dream. On the other hand, he may have just put another notch in his belt. To him, she is a one-and-done deal. That's what sex means to lots of men. So, ladies, don't mark your calendars yet. Ninety days might be a milestone for a job that might downsize or fire you one day, but marriage and sex are supposed to be until death separates you two.

No matter how people live today, God designed sex as His special ingredient for marriage. It's His secret sauce. Sex is for husbands and wives. That's what we've lost today: the longevity that comes with marital commitment. People seem to want only short-term involvements today. Hollywood marriages take a beating, and so does sex outside of marriage. Sex and money seem to run the world and everything in it. That's why you can't put a time limit on how long you wait, (or don't wait) to have sex. The average man can wait for years for sex from you, acting as your BFF while he's taking care of sexual business with LaQuita and Becky on the other side of town. *You don't hear me!* In fact, a real player can come and tighten you up every 90 days; so, you're going to need more than 90 days. You're going to need a man that serious about wife and family before sex, one that will stick and stay.

This is the big one. If his daddy was a player, you're probably going to be dealing with a man who is also a player, unless he's been changed by the power of God -- not changed by you, but by God. In fact, a real player can't help himself it's in his blood. So, ladies make sure you do a (BGC) *"back-ground check"* on old boy like he's applying for a government job, if not things can really get out of control.

It breaks my heart to see what women have come to at the hands of their men. Worse, women seem to be allowing themselves to be objects or toys rather than demanding to be treated with respect. Have you seen the dress code lately? **It's far freaking out!** Once upon a time, it seemed like the strip club was the place to go to pay money to see people drop it like it's hot! Not today. It seems like all you have to do today is wake up and go outside or turn on the TV, and you can see everything the whole *(kit-in-caboodle)* that most women used to keep to themselves: all of woman's glory on display for free. Now that's sad.

Yes, most of it is our fault, men. Instead of *covering* our women, we are *coveting* them. One of the biggest examples ever told of a man coveting a woman is found in 2nd Samuel 11. King David had one of his men killed because of a woman he coveted. He impregnated Bathsheba and attempted to cover up the pregnancy by convincing her husband to sleep with her on leave from military duty. When her husband refused to do so, David had him killed and married his wife Bathsheba. Even today, while women are watching their biological clocks and looking at the 90-day calendar, men are killing each other for sex.

The enemy is so deceptive, and we must stop falling victim to his schemes. Some of us wreck homes -- ours and others' -- with this sex thing. Then, in some cases, the homewreckers go on to get married, and live happily ever after in the new relationship that came from so much heartbreak. It's not right. *Enough is enough.* It must stop. There is no way we can carry on this way and leave our sisters behind at the hand of abusive relationships. Then some of us have the audacity to marry outside of the sisterhood. You abused her forever your (sister). I don't have a problem with you enjoying the varieties, and spice of life, I get it! put some of us take and give all our wealth away never to see it again, ask OJ. In some cases, women have carried men after having their kids for a long time, when the men were broken both ways, *(mentally and physically)* and down on their luck. Then those men left those same women alone to raise their children with no support from them. Can a Sista catch a break? A child said to me one day while in (children's church) when asked his father name, he said *"I don't have a daddy"* that broke my heart because we all have fathers he was just absent. This is a recurring situation that has bothered me to no end. It's bad enough to leave her with all those kids you helped produced (outside of the union), but then why do some men go and marry the Amy's and Becky's of this world?

I have yet to see the wealthy come down to the hood to marry Nook-Nook and Ray-Ray, but Becky gets a free ride. She has it made. That's why we must stop playing the sex card and try Jesus. Our women are being slaughtered and left behind alone. In too many cases, the kids just have to find their own way in the neighborhood. This pursuit of uncommitted sex must stop in favor of getting back to marriage and families. The biggest abuse out there with abandoned families are black. That's right, I said it. African-American women are taking a beating trying to find true love and families with their brothers. I feel your pain., I don't have all the answers but this one thing I know, when a person feels of know use they move on, and we don't want to lose the *Sista's hood.* We have problems that need to be fixed, but ladies please don't leave us!

Above anything else, Jesus is who we need to solve these problems! Not only did He die, and rise again, He gave you and me dominion over this earth. Read the Psalms 115:16, and Genesis 1:26. So ladies, forget about 90 days; let's talk about eternal days. If he's not talking marriage and family and want to have sex with you tell him to *"step to hell"* ahead of time, because the *"wages of sin is death...."* That's My Cure and response to sex outside of the union. I don't care how many days it's been. If he likes your sex, he should put a ring on it and own it. I know I've got to be helping somebody?

I've watched men, particularly black men, leave their wives to marry their mistresses and then divorce the former mistresses after having children with them. That mistress gets half of everything her former husband owns. I'm not mad at her getting half, I'm mad at her getting half of the first wife's millions and taking it back to (some) of their already wealthy families, making them richer in some cases. Meanwhile, on the south side of town, where the former husband was born and bred, his original family is getting poorer, never to see that money again.

Do you know how many families on the south side of town can use that type of support and move on up into high society? Something like George Jefferson, on up to the Eastside. The women who were left behind by these now successful men still live in those neglected neighborhoods. They are the women who were with those now successful men when they had nothing. It seems that most of the women these successful men marry from the other side of the tracks end up being their former wives anyway. Why didn't he marry Laquita, Shanita, or Lawanda then divorce her and let her enjoy that money, so she can take care of all those kids the now successful man left her with? I watch athletes come from the (hood), where their moms had *absolutely nothing*... and too many of them give their wealth away to other people. Why not bring that money home to your neighborhood, like the Hiltons, Rockefellers and Vanderbilt's do? That's the right thing to do; like all the other wealthy people of this world keeping their wealth in their neighborhoods. We have wealth, we just give it away having sex outside the union... to other people.... Besides, how can you love our athletes so much on the ball fields, and kill them walking the streets? This is how you make it and keep your wealth, so one day your neighborhood and families will have something. *Stop giving your wealth away for sex.* Did you know that the dollar bounces around 18 times among Jews, before it's leaves their community? Can you imagine where we would be as a race of people keeping that type of commitment with one another? With are talent and created minds, we would walk in *(kingship.) The way God intended us too!* Most of the women who end up married to and divorced from these wealthy men would have had sex with them for nothing. They didn't have to give them their wealth. If a man is going to have sex with someone, he should try to put his efforts back into his neighborhood and his family, so they can have something to look forward too, *recreations centers, schools, shopping malls, free outside events, etc.*... trust me it will keep crime down in the neighborhood. In the sex game, when you reach a certain status (fame/money) it's not sex anymore, it's a *(royal chess game)!* And the spoils go to the fittest.

That's the slaughter I'm talking about: woman being left alone with nothing, played like a game. Ladies, if you knew what I know, you would tell the playboy to go screw himself, because that's just what women are getting: Screwed! Ladies put it on lockdown and forget about getting paid dollars. Get paid millions like Becky. She marries him and gives him some babies, then she really screws him and gets half of everything. Don't believe me ask "Tiger." *Real talk.* If I only knew what he wanted. Look at all the girls with long straight hair getting paid, behind athletes from the hood; but when Ray Ray and OJ are broke running from the cops they come running back to the hood looking for help; not to the wealthy family they just made **richer**. It's time out. If you must screw him, *(I don't recommend it, outside the union)* screw him like Becky or Marsha and get paid. *Bishop Secular* has a radio show and said it's ok to be secular for two minutes.

Back to if I only knew what he wanted? ...

We all mess up, but now it's time to set the record straight and clean up what we messed up. There are guys out there we call OGs (old gangsters); guys with experience in life. We need their life lessons. It's time for them to sit down and stop trying to be players, because is time for them to give good, Godly advice and hopefully save a soul.

I asked for some advice one day from an OG and he almost jacked my life up concerning women telling me that the more women you have makes you a man. I put it in a poem entitled;

"Why You Tell Me That." I was a young man looking for knowledge, so I went to a grown man asking for manly advice on how to handle a woman. I expected him to tell me how to do this or that. What I got was useless misinformation from a misguided adult. Maybe his father had been like a compass with a broken needle, with *no north, south, east, or west.* So how could he advise me? With little experience myself, I moved forward on that broken compass advice and a life of diapers and milk began for me.

I mean, it's not like I was a virgin, but for the next move I was about to take after seeking grown folk's guidance I needed a man's advice on what to do when a woman *drops the linen and starts grinnin'.* I needed to know what I was in for. My motives were right, but my support system failed me. I found out later, but hopefully not too late; that being a man is not how many women you seduce, but how much you love the one woman you have. See, all I ever wanted was to be a family man with a wife, home, 2.5 children, a good job, and Christ in my life. Maybe it was my fault for seeking the advice of an OG; maybe I should have gotten some real Godly advice. Well, now I know.

Matthew 6:33 urges us to *"seek the kingdom of God first"*. Well, while I'm sharing, can you believe all I wanted to know from the OG was how to *"handle" a woman?* What was wrong with asking him that? Just make sure in life you never take a fool's advice, or a *"No"* from someone who doesn't have the authority to give you a *"Yes."* After research, trials, and error, I finally sought the Kingdom of God and its righteousness. Then He gave me the advice I had been looking for in all the wrong places. The Lord led me to the answer to my question: *how do I handle a woman?* The way you handle a woman, the Lord revealed to me, is to *love her, love her, love her!*

That's all I needed to know. That's all I was looking for. Can you believe all I wanted to know was how to handle a woman? Can you believe most guys really don't know that simple thing? Now I see why some women are so lost and don't know what he really wants from her. Sex is not the answer to loving a woman. The answer to loving a woman is to give yourself to her. Most men think this is a sign of weakness, but it's not. I'm 6'5," and weigh 265 pounds. I am an ex-ballplayer, and a North Carolina Golden Glove champion who fought on the National Golden Gloves boxing team in Albuquerque, New Mexico. And I had a hard head pretty much all my life. Physical strength and mental strength are two different things. Today I have mental strength ...and that's knowing the power of God and of Woman. I have learned that giving yourself to your woman is not a sign of weakness; it's a sign of strength. The key to that strength is found in the Basic- Instructions- Before- Leaving -Earth... yes, the Bible.

Ephesians 5:25 (ESV)
Husbands love your wives, as Christ loved the church and gave himself up for her,

Isn't that simple? Smile... I think this is where the problem is with relationships. We're getting information from the wrong sources: people with broken compasses. So, if we're going to help get our ladies back on track, we men must give ourselves back to them. Hear me, brothers, we are deeply indebted to the sisters. Remember that your mama is a sister. When nobody trusted you, or gave you a chance, she did. It was Laquita, and Lakeisha, who had your back, not Marsha. Therefore, women don't know what you want, because she gave you everything, and you still dumped her for someone who was never there for you. Other women found you when you were wealthy, or you found her. *(and gave her all your money), dummy...* Tanisha knew you when you were broke, and a joke. Didn't she? She fed you when you were hungry, with her government cheese from her state check. Yes, she did! Don't get grand now because you got paid. She dressed you when you didn't know how to match your clothes, let you live with her when your mama put you out, and gave you sex when your little worm got hard. Now you're moving on? I don't think so. Now, she needs you. She's lost and confused looking at a calendar hoping 90 days will be her cure all, in the relationship game. Wrong again. Ladies don't do it until he gives you his all or you'll just be a good screw. **Real talk.** One of the biggest mistake's women make is living with a man they are not married to. That trumps sex. It's bigger than sex. See the name it has? Trumps, it will try to win over you even if it must cheat, meaning living with you is bigger than just having sex. The place you rest is everything, after Jesus made the heavens and the earth He rested. Don't just let anybody come into your resting place.

Genesis 2:2 (ESV)
And on the seventh day God finished his work
that he had done, he rested on the seventh
day from all his work that he had done.

The chances you had for marriage were 100% when you were dating and visiting each other's house. When he moves in, you lose a great percentage for that chance. The suspense of dating gave you the upper hand. Once you move in unmarried; playing house, your chances for marriage just went way down. Point blank. Living together unmarried steals your advantage. You do everything a married woman does, without the benefits. Live-in girlfriends cook, clean, lay down, and stand up. The only thing the girlfriend gets that the wife doesn't get in the end is screwed! You better hear me and get on your feet and move out to your own place if you ever want matrimony. When it comes to material things, he should test them first, because we love test driving things. It's good to test drive cars, boats, and planes that's material things, but you don't test drive people's heart. That's what shacking is; **test driving.** Ray Parker, Jr. song, entitled, *"Let Me Go."* The song says, "if you're not sure that you want me, let me go." I can respect that, he said don't have me hanging on just in case. The thing most men don't know about ladies is that she's very gentle like a crate of eggs, or fine china; one bump or drop can break them all. Guys have been dropping women left and right, not knowing the wealth that is in their hands.

I'll never forget working long hours in the salon needing help. I would hire people only to find that I had to let them go. I got tired of working long hours alone. One morning I was getting dressed after a long day at the salon. I looked over at my wife still asleep...snoring, in fact. God showed me that all the help you need is laying right beside you every night. ***Well, rip my pants,*** that revelation was all it took for me. My wife and I have been working together ever since. I found out she was the answer to my success. God showed me that my wife is also my favor in this life.

Proverbs 18:22 (ESV)
He who finds a wife finds a good thing and
obtains favor from the Lord.

I was laying next to my success and favor from God, and didn't even know it, but now I do, and so do you. Maybe you'll hold your sweetheart a little closer and tighter now and, give her your name so you'll have instant favor with God. Please never mishandle or drop her again. Test drive all the material things you must, but never take your lady or spiritual things for granted. Your woman is the most spiritual gift you will ever possess, outside of the Holy Spirit. By possession I don't mean control or domination, but that you are fully responsible for her wellbeing.

Psalm 34:8 (ESV)
Oh, taste and see that the Lord is good!
Blessed is the man who takes refuge in him!

Psalm 34:8 describes the state of mind we all need to get back to and stay in. It's time to go back to the Old Landmark -- not to OGs who give us bad advice-- but God, who never fails.

Out of all the creations God made, only one, the most intelligent, wants to have intercourse with each other (same sex). This is extremely hard to talk about because I have family members that live that life style, but that don't stop me from telling the truth about Gods word or loving them. My #1 season for writing is to help people come to the knowledge of Christ and eternal life! not to stop you from having sex, either way! FYI I am a hairstylist by profession and have lots of friends that live that alternative life style. So not only does she not know what he wants, mankind is looking like it has lost its way also. If I only knew what he wanted? All the creatures from dinosaurs to caveman, knew who and what the right mate was for them. They knew what God meant when he said by fruitful and multiply. *This is a no brainer,* if you can't multiply with it Gods way, not test tub but embryo fruitfully through intercourse, everything else according to the bible is an abomination, according to Gods word.

I was watching a TV show one day and a woman introduced another woman as her wife. To each his own, the question remains. If that was her wife, what was she to her? Let me say this for the record, I'm not knocking anyone's lifestyle, and I'm not homophobic against homosexuals, in fact we need to know how to embrace the (GAY and L-G-B-T) community with the same love we have for one another. If you are mean to gays today you are so out of touch with Gods love, besides that's not my massage. I'm saying that if you follow, the Bible, and believe God's word, your lifestyle should have some type of resemblance to Christ, because this may not apply to you if you don't believe the Bible. Say what you want, but when you really love someone you tell them the truth, remember this in life, never… respect people that won't tell you the truth! I know you're scared to say it, so am I; just like I was when I called out the 90-day rule for having sex, but what do you do say Nothing? …and let Gods people and the people you say that you love to perish? If you think it's scary now, wait until JESUS RETURNS!

Many people won't read the Bible, so read this: *sin – all kinds -- sucks the life out of you.* It seems that most of the world's problems are because men never dominate the right dominion. God wants us to care for one another, not rule over one another. We were supposed to do this world together. Instead, we enslave one another, and that's our biggest problem. One group is always trying to rule everything and everybody, and that's not going to work. Men, if you want to rule, rule your house well, and love your wife. Most of your problems start and end right there any way. Right now, the woman doesn't know what she wants or needs, neither does the man, because they are trying to rule over one another.

I believe she would *"know what he wanted"* if he was in his place as the man of his home, but he's out doing who-knows-what-with-whomever, and she might be out now doing the same thing! I believe with all my heart that women want to do the right thing with their men, but for some reason, women seem shell shocked. Why? Because their men have dropped them so much that women have given up on men being in place.

I'm repenting for mankind. We must get it together. SOS is an international code signal for extreme distress. It is used by ships and planes to call for help. My brothers and sisters, we need help so I'm sending out an **SOS;** a call and request for help and rescue for mankind.

Ever since the Garden of Eden, man has been failing with woman. He came up short on his first assignment by eating fruit that God had forbidden him to taste. There was nothing wrong with eating fruit, it was <u>that</u> <u>fruit of that one tree</u>... and still today man is eating forbidden fruits.

People of God, we must pray hard because she doesn't know what he wants, and he evidently... *definitely, unequivocally, absolutely* ... doesn't know what she wants or needs. One thing I know is we all need God so that we can appreciate and understand the gifts we have in each other. We men must work double-time to put confidence back into women, so that they know their high value, and prime property they are.

When I talk with my wife about her teenage years H/S and M/S, she often tells me what guys liked and disliked in girls; silly things like *skin color and hair length. One group all liked girls with big breasts, and the other group liked girls with big butts,* nothing with subtend. When you're going through adolescence, being judged on such frivolous standards can kill your self-esteem, and that's what a lot of us guys did to the girls we interacted with. Some of us even went so far as to leave negative comments about our schoolmates telling them that they were fat and ugly.

So many women are still dealing with those hurts as adults. We must clean up those old conversations. We rarely tell our women how beautiful and precious they are with their *tan skin, or their beautiful brown eyes, their curly, straight, long, short, deep wavy, or shiny hair; or their thick juicy lips, pudgy noses.* We need to let our women know how much we appreciate them in their natural state, and what gifts they are to us. They need to know that they are simply altogether lovely just as they are.

I enjoy telling my wife that she is a beautiful Queen. My intention is to praise her -- not worship her, --because I only worship the Savior. Gentlemen, it's our job to affirm our women because we tore her down with our childish adolescent conversations about who they were and what they looked like.

Singer India Arie declared in one of her songs, *"I am not my hair" ...or my skin.* That's beautiful. But that's not her job, men are the reason so many women feel inadequate to operate at their potential. Men need to go back and set the record straight. Why because we go after the light, bright, damn-near-night, straight hair type after we make that money. What we prefer is showcased in our actions. When men celebrate the style of a certain type of woman they are saying all over again to other types of women that they're not good enough. Those are the things boys might have said to them when they were little girls. Today women are still trying to figure out what men want. Too many women lament that *"if I only knew what he wanted, maybe I could fix it."* The truth is the women never broke nothing. Men started those negative conversations, so it's our job to fix them. Gentlemen, if you care anything about mankind, encourage your women, first in your home and then in the streets. We jacked that up too by buying women! So, fix it! all the way from the bottom to the top so she can start believing in herself again, and maybe you too.

I have so many horror stories from women who talk about all the insults they endured from their male friends. I would love to charge some of these men with verbal abuse and see them punished for the crime of hurling devastating insults at these women. We must clean up what we have messed up, because all she ever wanted to do was please her man. I look at my wife sometimes and wonder aloud what men before me could have been thinking to let go of such a beautiful, priceless woman? I was honored that she gave me the opportunity to go out on the town with her. Then I toasted the fools who let her go. My wife dated me despite my past, and she knew a lot about me. I believe she knew what she wanted, and once I came in with a clear vision for us, the Spirit woman in her identified with the real deal in me.

Initially, she just wanted to date me, with no real expectations, because men she dated had failed her in the past, so dating was the top shelf for her, but not for me. Her top shelf was just going out having a good time, because most guys never took ownership, and showed her how she fit into the relationship, but I set the bar high. ***Real high.*** Most women don't know what guys want because there is no clear vision for them as a family.

Most guys just want sex. You've got to give your woman a vision of your future together; something to see, then she'll show you where the real sex is.

Remember, creatures have sex, but humans *make love*. I stopped just having sex when I met my wife. Lovemaking is the real deal. Love takes you to another level with your woman. I feel sorry for people in serious relationships who never experience the art of real lovemaking; crying, holding each other before and after; praying together while making love. It's a whole other world. Dogs have sex in public. That's not love. That's biology -- it is in their nature. Lovemaking is special, private, even sacred. Most people don't know about that. If you're just screwing, you could be a wrench; or a *screw-driver...* Lovemaking is sex at its highest level; it takes you into the cosmos of each other's emotions because while it only takes a minute to fall in love, it takes a lifetime to build on that love.

Because so many have embraced the thought that a woman should be a lady in public and a freak in the bedroom, some women don't know when to turn off the freak and be a lady. Now the freaks don't just come out at night; they're all over the place, day and night. Ladies, I recommend two things to you. First, get a personal relationship with the Master, Jesus Christ, so he can show you your Boaz -- a good man. Then love the person God made you to be: *not a freak, but a lady.* You are not who those boys said you were way back in high school, either. Men who want to be in committed relationships love a lady who knows who and whose she is. He may never know what you want, but he'll find out that he needs you when you showcase the lady that you are. Be the woman

God made you to be and watch him find you. If what you're living for is not worth Christ dying for, *who cares what the man wants*?

Chapter 8

Woman, You Are Anointed To Do This

Luke 1:26-27 (ESV)
Birth of Jesus Foretold
In the sixth month the angel Gabriel was sent
from God to a city of Galilee named Nazareth,
a virgin betrothed to a man whose name was
Joseph, of the house of David. And the virgin's
name was Mary.

It was only fitting that God chose the woman as the vessel to express his highest purpose in the earth. Part of God's master plan from the beginning was to prepare the woman's body to bring forth life. *"Who knew, especially Mary, that she would be God's choice for such a precious gift to the world?"* Isaiah 9:6 gives us a full description of this child coming, but when and how the child would come into the world was the mystery.

Isaiah 9:6 (ESV)
For to us a child is born, to us a son is
given; and the government shall be upon
his shoulder, and his name shall be called

Wonderful Counselor, Mighty God, Everlasting
Father, Prince of Peace.

When the angel came to Mary and said, *"You will have this child,"* she immediately responded with a legitimate question: *"How is this?"* After all, she was a virgin. The angel calms Mary's concerns by assuring her that God was the answer to her question. Isaiah's description of the child to come, many knew that sooner or later somebody would be chosen as the vessel to bring forth God's very highest purpose. After all, is anything too hard for God? Look who was used for God's ultimate expression in the earth: woman. Like Mary, you are anointed to do this. It was the woman who brought forth the *wonderful counselor, mighty God, everlasting Father, and prince of peace.* Now think about that just for a moment. If you, like the young Mary, have been blessed by God to bring that kind of power out of you, I can only wonder what kind of power you have left inside of you. That's why there are penalties for not being a lady first: God made you to bring forth Greatness. So, sleeping around with different men not only brings down your value, it also offsets your place in creation, as a mother to all on earth. What a high honor. The world was framed on God's word, but it came through you. Wow. Every great thing done on this earth you had a hand in on it. Wherever you find yourself, remember you are anointed to do it. When Isaiah said, *"unto us a child is born,"* right then and there, God had you in mind. Can you see more clearly now where you fit into the scheme of things in God's mind? He has placed you right next to greatness, which is why, like Mary, you can do what God has assigned you to do. The woman God would choose to give birth to his only son would be most blessed among women, but Mary wouldn't have known her purpose from the beginning. But God had his eyes on her as that somebody. God, the creator of everything, not only had Mary on his mind, but used her for this ultimate purpose, just as he has you in mind for a specific purpose. Remember when we would play hide and seek or tag? When the person found you, and tagged you, you were it. Then, you had to do the finding and the tagging. Not anymore. In God's eyes, you're it, so (Baby Doll) people are now looking for you, with permission from God Himself.

Proverbs 18:22 (ESV)
He who finds a wife finds a good thing and
obtains favor from the Lord.

Because you are favored among women, you have great value. The Bible says, *"a man that finds a wife finds a good thing and obtains favor from the Lord."* For so long, some women have thought so little of themselves, but you need to know how great you are. I find it very interesting that Adam came from the ground and God gave him authority to name things in the earthly realm. God also mentioned that He knew us before we were formed in our mothers' wombs. All that's great, but there's an unmentioned knowledge about the woman. The Bible gives us the intelligence that she came from the man, Adam and Adam came from the ground with a special knowledge from God to named everything. He named all the proper social rules for life to function on earth. The woman was anointed to help him, and she knew more about him than he knew about himself. Think about the power and the insight God gave women. Adam coming from the ground, he knew what the earth needed to survive. Likewise, ladies you came from the man, and God designed you to know what he needed to survive. While he was exploring earth, the woman was inside of Adam exploring him (metaphorically). *Here's the kicker,* if the man that supposed to know everything came from you that makes you? That's right, Queen of everything.

I was dealing with some money the other day and the numbers weren't adding up. *Have you ever had that problem with money?* I kept counting and the money kept coming up the same. Well, I had it in my head that the numbers were bigger, but that bigger amount wasn't in my hands... yet. So, I worked some numbers in my head and I noticed that the more zeros at the end of a whole number the greater your amount. For so long, women have been disrespected and disregarded by men in the world system, as if they are zeros. Well I came to let you know there's a great value in being a zero. If you want your money to add up to something greater, put some zeros on it.

I'm going to show you the power of the zero. Every great man this world ever had who walked in integrity had a woman at his side. Metaphorically; let's say the woman is a zero, the place God took her from out of Adam's side. FYI; the rib, happens to be in my Son and I opinion the best part of the meat on any animal, so just like that she came from zero too Hero.

I'm telling you if you want to be great in the things of God, find you a wife and treat her right, because just like the zero has no value by itself, it has great value when you put it next to a whole number. Your woman would have the same power in your life if you would give her some room to showcase her gifts: she will add even greater value to your existence. A zero by itself has no value, except on a thermometer, that's the power of a zero. A zero in the right place can make things greater and greater. Put a one to the left of a zero you have $10, to the right you have 0.1cents. In other words, gentlemen, put your woman in the right place, the same place the Creator brought her from your side, and the quality of your life will improve, while your temperature rise as well, as your bank account.

God chose Mary for bearing and rearing; she was the one who would give birth to the savior of the world. If Mary brought the Savior into the world, just think what your wife can do with your world. Look at woman's handiwork being on God's team. Her work was on the A-list.

Let's look at her resume, and the great work she has done. Look how woman are showcased throughout the Bible. For example, there was a dispute in the Bible about who a certain child belonged to. Solomon had to make a difficult decision, because two women were claiming the same baby.

> **1 Kings 3:20-21 (ESV)**
> *And she arose at midnight and took my son from beside me, while your servant slept, and laid him at her breast, and laid her dead son at my breast. When I rose in the morning to nurse my child, behold, he was dead. But when I looked at him closely in the morning, behold, he was not the child that I had borne."*

Solomon, immediately commanded that the baby be cut in half and give half to each woman, but the true mother screamed, please don't kill my son. That woman showcased her strength under the worst conditions and saved her child's life.

When the walls fell in Jericho, the people went into the city and took control of it, destroying all that was in the city: men, women, ox, and sheep. But there was one woman named Rahab, a harlot who kept her family and herself alive, and all her father's household, all because she hid the spies disguised as messengers. People really looked down on Rahab like she was a zero, because she was a (prostitute) but she saved her father's whole household.

Women, you are anointed to do whatever God has appointed you to do. I bet she doesn't look like a zero now. She looks more like a Hero, all she needs is to be in the right situations and she will perform great things. When the King ordered someone to be killed, that person and his or her entire household were wiped off the face of the earth forever. But Rahab saved not only her life, but her family's name, because she was anointed.

When Jesus was on the cross look who was there at His lowest place of His ministry: four anointed women watched him suffer. They couldn't stop the persecution, but they refused to let him suffer alone. I like the way women think, she's on stoppable something like seeds, they grow under and in any conditions, give seeds some room and they will grow throw a rock.

John 19:25 (ESV)
but standing by the cross of Jesus were his

mother and his mother's sister, Mary the wife
of Clopas, and Mary Magdalene.

Their own danger or sadness of the spectacle and the insults from the people didn't stop them from performing the last official office of duty to show tenderness and love to their Lord. These women were on the scene despite any trouble they have faced. Today, women are still on the scene in the most difficult places as helpmates; as anointed vessels, acting as arteries in the body; carrying blood supply from the heart to all the parts of the body. Today, it's the woman still carrying, caring, and saving lives, like she did with the *(umbilical cord)* before child birth with the right nutrition for life, supporting people and things in its infant places. You truly are God's chosen vessel for his highest expression in the earth. You are anointed for this, because you know the value of the zero. Who else comes through for someone when he is down on his luck? You, the woman.

The greatest example is found, when the Angel Gabriel came to her about the virgin birth.

Luke 1:30-31 (ESV)
And the angel said to her, "Do not be afraid,
Mary, for you have found favor with God. And
behold, you will conceive in your womb and
bear a son, and you shall call his name Jesus.

Luke 1:38 (ESV)
And Mary said, "Behold, I am the

servant of the Lord; let it be to me
according to your word."

Can you imagine the insight you must have with God, and the Holy Spirit to go for a deal like that? Let me put it in everyday language. *(Honey)*, I'm pregnant by the wind, (holy spirit). Trust me woman know things most men will never know, don't believe me try to tell a man that he has a child with a woman that he never had sex with, some don't clam the one he knows is his child, so you know a woman he was never with don't stand a chance.

I used to wonder why women always seem to go into relationships with men who don't deserve them? My sisters for instance, would get on my nerves finding every jail bird, drug dealer, or user, for their boyfriends. I never understood why, now I know why. I still don't approve, but I get it. Women are anointed to help. That's why God called you the (help meet, or helpmate) in modern English. Women see things differently than men, it's called a mother's love or intuition, every thought you ever had she saw it inside of you first as the rib cage. When the babies with the stinky diapers and snotty nose need to be cleaned, most men go the other way from the baby. On the other hand, women go to the baby with the stinky diaper and start kissing the baby with the snotty nose. She's anointed to work in all kind of stinky jobs. When my sisters were taking in zeros, or so I thought, they were not looking at what others saw with their physical eyes; they had x-ray vision, like God to see or examine what was in their man's spirit. When you have x-ray vision you can see things others can't. Maybe women have that x-ray vision, or maybe it's because the first woman once lived inside of the first man, disguised as the rib and knew what was really going on in the inside of man.

Be as it may, I owe my sisters an apology. I'm sorry, because when Jesus saw me, he looked beyond my faults and saw my needs. Thank God for x-ray vision. Most women are dealing with men who don't look right for the part. What she is trying to do is treat him, before he gets too bad. Like a doctor treats sickness in advance, the woman is trying to help despite what it looks like. I used to see women with guys and say, *"she can do better than that!* "Yes, she can, but she is anointed to do what you or I can't. We see jackass and zeros in some men, but she sees Boaz, and the potential of what could be. I don't know how, but she does. He has no car; home or job. She sees a Millionaire, and I see a panhandler looking for some woman to get over on and a place to lay his head. Women see what most people can't: God's favor on men others see as hopeless. I think she's just the softer side to men. Because of Rahab, the spies were not seen as spies, but messengers from God. Because of the woman fighting over the one baby she didn't see my child, but a child of God, and the baby was not cut in half. See what the anointing does? Because of Mary and the other women at the cross, Jesus didn't just die a lonely death, but He had company and rose again with all power in His hands. Not only do women save lives on earth, but it was a woman who saved the life of the one who gave eternal life to all who believe. You are anointed to do whatever God has prepared you to do, from the beginning of time, even for bearing and rearing the one who would be the Savior of the world. *Ladies, job well done.*

I believe it's time to celebrate you throughout the world, so get ready. It's your time. Mary, a woman of faith, responded with alarm when an angel of the Lord told her she had found favor with God and would give birth to the baby Jesus. She said, *How could it be, I'm a virgin?* That was a legitimate response. The thing we need to get out of Mary's response is God wants to bring greatness out of you from a clean vessel, but you first must stop letting people contaminate you with their *stuff and junk.* You are anointed for greatness. I don't know how you're going to top bringing the Savior into the world, but I know you will.

John 14:12 (ESV)
"Truly, truly, I say to you, whoever believes in me will also do the works that I do; and greater works than these will he do,

God is not through with you yet, because with God all things are possible. He has chosen you and needed you as the one to give birth to his son. **Selah.** Think about that for a moment. This is not like choosing a house, or a car or the suit you want to wear to the ball. This is the person who would carry the Savior of the world. Look how much God must love and believe in you. You don't just let anybody drive your car or hold your money. Even more powerfully, God was choosing the woman who would carry the world changer. We use the phrase "game-changer," but when someone knows all the answers to life that's a big deal. Women you need to know this. You're a *Game- Changer.*

From now on, your response to greatness when it comes, is *"Lord, I'm your servant. May everything you say come true in my life, whatever it is,"* because You have anointed me for this. For what, you ask? For whatever life brings your way. The Angel Gabriel's greeting to Mary wasn't an invitation or request; it was the grace and favor of God extended to her.

Have you ever been told there is greatness upon your life? But in that particular season in your life you could not see it; having no indication as to what you have been told, or what you believed; or any sign as to what God is doing. If you answered yes, you are favored -- highly favored -- among women, because God gave you grace, which is unmerited divine assistance given to us for regeneration and spiritual renewal. My sisters, God has put you in a place of regeneration to make you over, if needed. When people in life let you down and hurt you, or the pain of life finds you incomplete, God will just regenerate you. Trouble can't last always. Even though trouble comes, it can't stay. Not only can your body bring life, it also can renew and restore life. With that said, you don't have to understand the greatness in you; just believe and accept it.

The next time a divine angel comes to you with a great idea, just say, *"let it be done."* You're not a season, you're mother earth: the vehicle to bring forth life. You make the seasons; the seasons don't make you. That's why Jeremiah 29:11 said, *"I know the plans I have for you."*

What it doesn't say is, *"He has no idea,"* because He does. What happened to Mary is what I call preferential treatment. She received special favor not offered to everyone, but only to a select few. *Isn't that enough to shout about?* The anointing in your life put you among the few. Preferential treatment causes people and life to treat you better than others, for no certain reason. While I'm writing I'm almost jealous of the anointing in your life's ladies. Why? Preferential treatment sets you apart. You have been chosen by God to bring life into the world, and in Mary's case, to give birth to the Savior of the world. You're doubly blessed.

I believe the woman God gave to man is the most precious gift a person can ever have, above all the money, because nothing is better than favor. What you don't have, when you touch and agree with her because of that *(favor)*, the anointing in her life will bring it to pass. Man, you better find a wife quit!

Ladies, there's something God found in you that He couldn't find anywhere else. After all, He made you. God the Creator of heaven and earth couldn't find anyone or anything to do what you do. What you do is special, different from what is normal; and it is unusual in a good way. Like a newborn, women get special treatment. Gentlemen, if God, the Creator of all, thought enough to give women special treatment, we had better step up our game.

While Mary was fearful and troubled in the presence of the angel, she never expected to receive this kind of news. Ladies, I'm trying to prepare you for an explosion of blessings coming your way when you do God's will for your life, you're already chosen. God is trying to get all your stuff back to you. Get everything out of the way that doesn't give God glory. Joseph, Mary's husband, was about to hear some news that would come from God's Angels: Mary was favored. The same favor applies to you, ladies. ***Yes, you.*** Your pregnancy, though it may be unplanned to you, it's something that God knows all about. Ladies love all the *"oops babies"* just the same. God is going to regenerate you and the child, even though you have great honor and a great call on your life. There will also be great suffering as well but keep hope alive, there will be glory afterward.

1 Peter 5:10 (ESV)
And after you have suffered a little while, the God of all grace, who has called you to his eternal glory in Christ, will himself restore, confirm, strengthen, and establish you.

This scripture declares that after you suffer a while, God will establish you. Therefore, the things God is going to do for His chosen vessel are perfect. He is going *to establish, strengthen,* and *settle* you. I'm excited about all of them, but there is something special about being settled. Let's look at what God is going to do for those who suffer a little while, not for long, but a little while. First, He's going to *(perfect)* you like a doctor setting a broken bone. God will mend all your hurt and broken limbs; not just your broken hearts, but your lives, and make you whole again.

Next, He's going to *(establish)* you, which means God is going to make your way stable and straight. Despite the instability we face living in a world that inflicts suffering upon us all, God is going to call someone or something to make you widely known and accepted. Then, He's going to *(strengthen)* you like never before. You think Sampson was strong? You're going to have supernatural strength, unable to be explained by signs or laws of nature. The things that used to knock you down will have no effect on you today. God is going to give you the ability to succeed under all kinds of pressure, in all that you do for Him. Please note not for the world, but for Him. Are you shouting yet?

Then, He's going to *(settle)* you. To protect you against attacks from the enemy, God will build a firm foundation in you and make you steadfast and unmovable. That may not sound like much to you, but when a tree is planted by the water it never stops growing. That's what God is saying: you will be planted, not buried. When something has been buried, it's hidden or concealed, but when something is planted, it's to be revealed to make something that was secret or hidden, public. Anointed ladies get ready! God has planted you in Adam and the seed in you is about to grow. You can do nothing but grow into whatever you want to be; whether it's carrying the King of kings or being a help-meet to **Nuk-Nuk and 'em.**

You are anointed to do it, just like Mary. God called her to carry this anointing. It didn't mean her journey was going to be easy, but like Mary, you are going to win. One would think Mary didn't have the qualities or class to carry the Lord of lords. She was a young and poor country girl, but she had greatness inside of her, watered by faith. In the eyes of the people, she was only fit to be a wife or a mother, but never to carry King Jesus.

Ladies, people will always try to belittle or minimize your potential, so remember if they're not talking about great things, concerning you, they're not talking about you! Today, we minimize women who carry the favor of God as if His favor is a small thing, but she holds the favor and success for mankind. You have already been battle-tested Kings tried to kill you. Remember King Herod?

Matthew 2:8 (ESV)
And he sent them to Bethlehem, saying,
"Go and search diligently for the child, and
when you have found him, bring me word,
that I too may come and worship him."

His goal was to find you, Joseph, and baby Jesus and kill Him, but you carried and protected the King of kings. Remember, your family arranged for you to be married, thinking all you would be is just a good wife? And you were, but who would have imagined you would be carrying the King of kings? Mary worked and served hard. She also loved God, but hold on there's more to her, just like there is more to you than even you can see. All people see sometimes is your hard work, but they don't know what you're carrying. That's why the Bible says to *"be careful how you entertain strangers, you might be entertaining angels unaware."*

My wife, in my opinion is carrying the keys to life, as far as helping people especially young people. I can't wait until God reveals her many gifts. People see her work and the glory in her life, but they don't know her *story behind the glory.* Right now, my wife and I are attending a church, working faithfully anointed, just not appointed, but when God is ready, the world will know that she and I have been infected in a good way by God.

Did you know you can be in the perfect will of God, and still be in a hard place? *Ask Jesus and His disciples running for their lives.* I'm sure that during this time while Mary was awaiting the arrival of this great blessing, she had times of loneliness and feelings of rejection and uncertainty. Surely, she wondered what was going to happen and what people would think about her having a child *(baby daddy)* before she was married. Ladies have no fear, just like Joseph covered Mary, God is going to carry and cover you. Joseph didn't divorce Mary on the grounds of infidelity but kept the conception private. God is going to keep you private until the time is right. You may be thinking God has forgotten about you, but no; He's *concealing* you, keeping you out of sight for such a time as this. Just like wine stored in the cellar, you're about to be served at the King's table. I'm sure Mary was reluctant, and people doubted what she was carrying. They didn't realize she was carrying greatness. Woman of God, people see one thing in you --the sum; but God sees the whole. People never see the greatness in your life, but God sees all. We all need to thank God that people can't determine the outcome of your struggles. Brother Joseph (Israel's son) was in the center of God's will, and at the same time in a pit. Again, he was in the center of God's will, then was put in prison. Sometimes you can be carrying greatness and feel like you're stuck in the mud struggling. Isn't it funny how God will put you where they think you need to be? I'm starting to think hard places are designed to push you out, **like up, up, and away,** to the greatness God has in store for you.

Joseph was not just in any man's house. He was placed in Potiphar's house, a royal place. God brought him from the prison to the palace. The place you're in right now is not permanent, lasting, or continuing for a very long time, and definitely not forever. It's not God will for your life. Your wilderness is not permanent. The anointing in your life is working on your behalf. As (Sam Cook) sang, *"It's been a long time coming, but, a change is gonna come."*

During some of your difficult times, you must recognize where God has placed you. Because we're anointed, the place where my wife and I serve now, we found ourselves not being used at all... the way we thought we would, being anointed, ordained, season and on fire for the Lord. But we found out, it's a place for us to learn, serve, develop more and oversee our feelings. We are learning how to take classes in the Christian arena, so we can continue to grow. Most Christians don't know it, but they're underdeveloped. They can preach, but so can a parrot. *"Polly, want a cracker"* And like a parrot, an underdeveloped Christian can't live the life he or she preaches about. Most importantly, we're learning how to serve with integrity. For me it's like going to seminary. My day is coming! Sometimes, success involves struggles, and advancement sometimes comes from adversity. So, remember this: the anointing is going to cost you something.

Joseph probably had no idea why he had to experience persecution, especially from his brothers. When you are anointed, it seems like trouble comes from every direction. I'll never forget 1Samuel 19:9 when Saul tried to kill David. An evil spirit came on Saul, and he tried to pin David to the wall with the javelin spear.

1 Samuel 19:9-10 (ESV)
Then a harmful spirit from the Lord came
upon Saul, as he sat in his house with his
spear in his hand. And David was playing the
lyre. And Saul sought to pin David to the wall
with the spear, but he eluded Saul, so that he
struck the spear into the wall. And David fled
and escaped that night.

Ladies, because you are so anointed and favored by God, even people you think are with you will fail you or try to take your position or life. Don't be hurt and fall out with them, because you are anointed to regenerate and to survive. The things that kill most can't touch you. Mary probably wondered why, just like you, that God would allow her to be ostracized and talked about, then still carry this type of anointing (Jesus). Look at God ... Mary was the (prototype, an original), our first model of something from which other forms or copies are developed. The original model is something from which something is patented. It is the mold for a repeated pattern or design.

Ladies, you are God's chosen vessel for God highest expression into eternal life. You can't lose. *Talk about a secret agent.* God created you at the same time He created Adam but wouldn't let you come on the scene until the coast was clear, to protect you from all hurt, harm, and danger. Even though you go through things, you can't lose. When you carry this type of anointing, sometimes you must learn how to encourage yourself, as well as have a made-up mind in the things of God, and know who God made you to be, even in the lowest places on earth.

Women find a way to rise. Who else makes comebacks like the sisters? You can't be who you were and who God is calling you to be at the same time. Ladies, when you're carrying this type of seed, you're carrying abundant life, It's all about the seed. Women you are anointed for this: to speak life out of hard places. I'm sure Mary spoke to her baby, that's what pregnant women do: speak greatness to what they are carrying, babies big or small. Oh yes, Mary was more than just the vessel, she had a hand in speaking life to Jesus. What an honor. So, ladies whenever you think you're losing, just open your mouth and speak life, because your *mouth is bigger than your mountains.* You're anointed. Remember what God has placed inside of you from day one: The King of kings, and Lord of lords. You not only carried the one with all power, God gave you the power to use on credit. Ladies, you have power to the second power because you carried the ultimate power -- Jesus -- then God gave that power to you and me. Whenever your back is up against the wall, remind yourself like the Shunamite woman: *"All is well."*

2 Kings 4:23 (ESV)
And he said, "Why will you go to him today? It is neither new moon nor Sabbath." She said, "All is well."

This had to be the most amazing story I ever heard, about a woman that had super faith. After her son dies on her lap, she places her son on the bed and want to look for the man of God. When her husband and friends ask her is everything okay leaving the house, all she said was *"It shall be well."*

That is our new declaration from now on, on the mountains of life or in the valleys, however you find me, when asked: *"All is well."*

You are anointed to do this! Regardless of what happens in your life, it shall be well. You must remember you carried the King, the anointed one. Ladies you destroy the yokes in life, whatever it is. Because you are anointed to do this!

Chapter 9

Extraordinary You

When I think about great people in this world, my first thought is Mama. Most people would say a doctor that saved life's or an inventor that advanced the way we live today, that great but in the face of mama it's just another *(days of our lives as the world turns)*. My mother she's extraordinary. She reared, nurtured, and encouraged nine kids and a host of grandchildren. She deserves a special award. She had a special way of keeping us together like magnets. I hope that was your first thought of greatness also your mama. Most people think about men who did this or that great thing, and that's okay. But I'm here to inform you about a great and extraordinary woman who not only kept God's commandment to be fruitful and multiply, but she also saved mankind. A woman, much like extraordinary you, has a place in the Hall of Fame in the Kingdom of God. I can't help to think where man would be without his helpmate. A woman, one much like extraordinary you, saved the world when she yielded her body to allow the King of kings, and Lord of lords to borrow her body to be the vessel for safe entry into the world; so, it's you today we are honoring... Extraordinary you.

I like Maya Angelou's descriptions in *"Phenomenal Woman."* Angelou talks about herself – and, most importantly, all women -- using strong, affirming language, including: *"Men themselves have wondered what they see in me. They try so much, but they can't touch my inner mystery."* When I think about woman and the power she possesses, she has to be the most amazing person ever. Just think of all a mother do to keep the life of her family in balance. Circus clowns drop stuff all the time juggling, but not mama, none of her babies ever hit the ground, nor does she drop a child accidentally from her arms. A mother is a master juggler when it comes to family. First, she carries the baby inside her until it is born; then she feeds and nurses the baby. Then raises the child, all the while – in many cases-- taking care of her big child, her man. With all of what she does as a mother and helpmeet, she has to be the most extraordinary ever. Many men do one or two things to care for a child, in some cases, that one thing is to help make the child by planting the seed.

My wife is a great example of a phenomenal woman. She does things I would not even think of doing for our son. Oh yes, I love him, but as far as I'm concerned, if he's not feeling well in the middle of the night, I could wait until well into the next morning to wake up and check on him. On the other hand, my wife will get up in the middle of the night because he's thirsty. Me too. As for me, I'd say too bad. He's thirsty; I'm sleepy. He can drink in the morning, and I'll drink with him.

I want to talk about some women who are extraordinary, like you and Mary, the mother of our Lord and Savior Jesus Christ. I can only imagine what was on Mary's mind when she found herself a pregnant virgin. The anxiety and the pressure alone had to be overwhelming, but that extraordinary woman took care of business. Not only did she carry, give birth to and care for Christ, she also did as God decreed and named him Jesus. Now just for the record, when a woman carries a child 9 month, you don't tell her what to do with her child or what to name that child. Nobody on earth has that much clout, but the Savior.

Matthew 1:23 (ESV)
"Behold, the virgin shall conceive and bear a
son, "and they shall call his name Immanuel"
(which means, God with us).

After all, Mary was a little shy country girl she could've had five names for the child, his name could have been *Bubba, William, Rudolph, Earl, Thomas the III* ... Because Mary was extraordinary, not ordinary, she carried out God's plan and named the child as the prophet had foretold.

Luke 2:11 (ESV)
For unto you is born this day in the city of
David a Savior, who is Christ the Lord.

There are certain things you must know and commit to doing no matter what limitations, barriers, oppositions, or challenges confront you. You know the whole town was talking about her, but she took care of the child and followed through like only an extraordinary woman could. Mary's situation had to be heart-wrenching for her, to say the least: she was pregnant and had never known a man sexually. That alone for most people would be a (deal-breaker) concerning marriage. I almost want to take my hat off to brother Joseph also, after all that was his lady (smile)... And she's pregnant and he known he was not the father sexual. In most households that's a fight, with pending funeral arrangements all by itself... Yet, Mary, the mother of Jesus, followed through with God's plan for their lives. Can you imagine what the world would be like if we were to hear God and follow through on what He gives us to do? I would venture to say half of our problems would be over, but that wouldn't be the complete truth: we probably wouldn't have No problems. We would have victory's all the time. Most of the trouble we get into is because we hear God, but don't follow through on what He reveals to us. Thank God for extraordinary Mary.

1 Corinthians 15:57 (ESV)
But thanks be to God, who gives us the victory
through our Lord Jesus Christ.

Another extraordinary woman is Rahab the prostitute. She hid the spies that was sent to scope out Jericho. She was a brave woman because she would have been in big trouble if she had been caught lying to the authorities. Her whole family would have been wiped off the face of the earth. But that extraordinary woman stood strong and took care of business. Her one act helped bring the walls of Jericho down and save the lives of many people. That's extraordinary.

Many of us today will sell a friend out much like Judas did Jesus for chicken change, but this extraordinary woman saw the bigger picture and helped out; not just herself and her family, but the Israelites and their community as well... What she did was tell a flat-out lie. The Bible clearly condemns lying throughout the Old and New Testaments. That's for the record. But her actions made her part of God's people, as in the ancestry line of David and Jesus. Her life was also part of a conquest of Canaan -- the promised land -- a task that God commissioned and blessed. Does her example mean that lying can sometimes be an acceptable course of action? In Rahab's case, there are two possibilities: either her lie was not a sin, or it was a sin. If it was a sin, was it *excusable or inexcusable?* Those who say her lie was not a sin would sometimes say they believe the loving thing is all that matters. A little lie in the name of love is no sin. In fact, it's the right thing to do. Whatever it was, it took a lot of courage from an extraordinary person. In this case, preserving the life of the spies had a higher value than the truth.

Wow. Rahab's deed sounds a little like what our Lord and Savior did for us. The Word of God says while we were yet in sin, Jesus gave his life and kept us from eternal death. In other words, He covered us just like our sins never happened. I hate to put Rahab on the same level as Christ, but this woman saved lives from extinction, which is what would have happened to the people if she had not lied. What Rahab did was beyond extraordinary. The Bible calls Rahab a prostitute, that somehow did the God thing what a conflicting situation, that's why we should never count no one out especially an extraordinary woman as you can see. We are not meant to take the positive results of Rahab's lie as an endorsement of the immoral aspects of her life. Like the rest of us, Rahab had a mixed character like some of us *"sometimes you feel like a nut, sometimes you don't"* but she believed in

God and honored him and his people. She was a great heroine; a woman who is admired for great and brave acts of fine quality. She came from the most surprising place -- Jericho -- the same Jericho where Jesus was baptized in the Jordan river by John the Baptist. Later, her name would be honored, not only for what she did for Israel but for what she became: a mother in the line of Jesus Christ. She was an extraordinary person.

You can't overlook another extraordinary woman, Elizabeth, the mother of John the Baptist, the one who baptized Jesus. First of all, she was both barren and advanced in age. That she gave birth to John is extraordinary all by itself. Her husband was advanced in age, so the last thing on their minds was to have a child in diapers. Nevertheless, the angel of the Lord appeared to her husband Zechariah and said to him, "Your prayers have been heard and your wife Elizabeth will bear a son." When Zechariah told his wife what the angel had said, she believed God's promise to them. Believing is all Jesus asks us to do in this life concerning His Word -- just believe. Elizabeth's belief and her faith is what made her extraordinary. Her husband Zechariah, on the other hand, became mute because he did not believe.

In the times we are living in now, there's no time to doubt. When the angel Gabriel told Mary that the Lord had chosen her to bring Jesus into the world, all she said was, *"Let it be according to your word."* She exhibited extraordinary faith at the highest level. As for Elizabeth, can you imagine what level of faith she had to have to bear a child in her nineties? Like these extraordinary women, God has also chosen you to be extraordinary you.

In the archives of extraordinary women, we have to mention Ruth and Naomi again as they travel from Judah to Moab where the favor of God met them. If you're going to be great in the things of God you must own two things in your spirit man, *believe and be consistent Ruth* was a great example. You almost can't talk about one without the other. Ruth was so extraordinary she has her own book in the bible that tells of her extraordinary greatness. One of the first things I noticed about Ruth is she has her own mind and her focus is on God. She recognizes greatness, because most people move to a new family with the hope of being wifey one day again, if they have sons but not Ruth. On top of that, Naomi, had to be anointed because extraordinary people don't follow losers. The other sister-in-law went back to her people, but Ruth stayed with Naomi. You might say what's so extraordinary about that? Well I'm glad you asked. Most people need a map to find hidden treasure. Extraordinary people just need to hear your heartbeat. That's right... That's why Orpah's story ended and Ruth's is from generation to generation. This is the extraordinary in you able to detect deep treasure in people. Orpah did the expected thing and returned home; yet Ruth unexpectedly stayed with her impoverish mother-in-law. Yes, she did. This is the reason why you don't count anyone out, especially a woman. What Orpah did was understandable, but not extraordinary. Orpah's actions meant that she left the Israelites and their God. On the other hand, Ruth stayed in the pocket like a master musician keeping the temple doing the tango are two step. This is where the extraordinary you come into play, along with the faith factor.

Ruth 1:16 (ESV)
But Ruth said, "Do not urge me to leave you
or to return from following you. For where
you go I will go, and where you lodge I will
lodge. Your people shall be my people, and
your God my God.

This was a beautiful and emotional moment of poetry. Ruth's assertion that Naomi's God would be her God is especially striking, because the law of Moses did not prohibit Israelites men from marrying Moabite women. That let us know that her motive was clear. She was not only clinging to Naomi's people and land, but also to Naomi's God. Ruth was willing to forsake all that she had ever known to follow the one true God. She was following in the footsteps of Abraham, who had forsaken his family and his homeland as well in response to God's command. When you move in this extraordinary way, God and God alone will put Boaz, Kings and Queens, right in your lap. This is how the story goes.

Ruth 2:1 (ESV)
Now Naomi had a relative of her husband's,
a worthy man of the clan of Elimelech, whose
name was Boaz.

Boaz was related to Naomi's husband Elimelech, and Boaz was a man of great wealth, land, produce and resources. Because she was extraordinary Ruth and Naomi's distressed situation put them in the middle of great men. Look at God working for his extraordinary woman.

Ruth became a part of Jesus's lineage because she walked in God's favor.

Solomon begat Boaz and Boaz begat Obed, Obed begat Jesse and Jesse begat David and David's bloodline was of the Messiah.

An extraordinary woman made her way from gleaning – gathering leftover grain -- in the field to owning the field all because she refused to live an ordinary life. Remember Ike and Tina Turner? Another extraordinary woman. All she wanted to keep out of the whole relationship was her name. Ike had all the ideas, but it was Tina that brought them to life… that's right extraordinary You. Ike saw in *(black and white)*, but Tina put it in color, when Tina left the Ike and Tina Revue, so did the show.

That's extraordinary you. Like Ruth, you must refuse to live a life beneath your potential. I have other example's of great woman you need to know about, like Sarai.

Genesis 11:30 (ESV)
Now Sarai was barren; she had no child.

Think about Sarah, the barren wife of Abraham. There is so much happening here. First, she encouraged her husband Abraham to lay with her maidservant Hagar because she was barren. Then she laughed at God's promise that she would have a child in her old age. I like Sarah because she could have just given up, but instead, she tried to intervene by giving Hagar to her husband and her husband obliged her, so they could have a child. What a legitimate screw, Y'all forgive me, but it was for the first-time old Abraham listened to his wife! Sarah was extraordinary, but didn't think the whole thing out. Who would go that far to aid in helping God's covenant come to pass? It's hard enough for a woman of childbearing age to carry a child for nine months; so, for a **90-year-old woman** to carry a child, she was not only extraordinary, she was committed to the promise, *and maybe a touch of delirious* **and a spot of delusional.** Smile... Once Sarah heard the promise, she wanted to get involved, unlike Jonah who ran fast.

Jonah 1:2-3 (ESV)
"Arise, go to Nineveh, that great city, and call out against it, for their evil has come up before me." But Jonah rose to flee to Tarshish from the presence of the Lord.

Sarah threw herself into God's plans and wanted to help out, though not in the way God planned. Like Rahab, who lied with an explanation, Sarah tried to do something. That's what extraordinary people do; they get involved. Sarah's laugh was not a laugh of doubt, but a laugh of delight, as if she was saying, *"what took you so long?"*

I'm convinced that women run the world -- the earth and all the people in it. *(Look at Mother Nature, she has her hand in on everything).* I know it's hard to digest, so take it in pieces. They are extraordinary! Extraordinary women are like flashlights in a blackout, getting us through the dark places of life by allowing us to see our way. The most extraordinary person of all time is God the Father and his Son Jesus. God used the woman after Jesus, He used His son to save the world and extraordinary you to fill it, that's the level you're on. I know people don't want to say it, but you're just like God with a little g. Don't let this scare you. The book of John gives us the intelligence as we search the scripture, that we find extraordinary is who we are, and ***Baby Doll*** you're at the top. (here's two for you to keep in your archive)

1 John 4:17 (ESV)
By this is love perfected with us, so that we may have confidence for the day of judgment, because as he is so are we in this world.

1 John 4:4 (ESV)
Little children, you are from God and have overcome them, for he who is in you is greater than he who is in the world.

You're just as God. As He is, so are we in this world. As we study Jesus' life, we clearly see that He was extraordinary as a teacher, leader, healer, deliverer, and worker of tremendous and countless miracles. He was a priest and prophet. He even had the ability to love and forgive those who murdered his flesh even though He was innocent. That's extraordinary beyond human understanding. Ladies, carefully study what God's word says about those who are born again, saved, and spirit-filled. Kingdom heirs show that we have been transformed into identicalness with our Lord and Savior Jesus Christ, which puts us in the category of being ordained by God as extraordinary. Ladies, you are moving into extraordinary greatness unfortunately, some guys just don't know who they're dealing with.

Men need to realize that their women are extraordinary because of God's favor. I used to be a womanizer until I came to the realization that I was not getting over the women I was having sex with; they were getting over on me. I came to the realization that my sperm to women was like gas to a car for it to go. When I realized my value and the value of my sperm, condoms became my best friend. *(Not to glorify the uses of condoms)* I understood that I had a responsibility to plant my seed in the right ground. Until a man comes to the knowledge of what his sperm could be, he'll just keep giving it away to anybody, but when he thinks about what that sperm could be when paired with the right egg -- presidents, great athletes, scientists, doctors who cure human diseases and prolong human life, book writers, the next *Nelson Mandela, or Barak Obama* (well maybe not them)… one in a lifetime, smile… When you know that, neither a man nor a woman should have any limitations. Until you come to that knowledge, you're just ordinary, doing ordinary things.

There's nothing wrong with ordinary. but women you must realize that you are the *(crème de la crème)*. Ordinary is not what you were made for you are extraordinary. In other words, you add the (extra) to ordinary. God show me what the problem was with (mankind). Because we're not *(Gemologist)* specialist in gems… Most of us don't know what a diamond looks like when it is unrefined, or in the rough. So, we throw good stuff and people away, not knowing the value of it.

We all need to realize and declare our likeness to Jesus and begin to leap over the limitations that life places on us. We need to run in pursuit of our God-ordained destiny. Our destiny contains things that we haven't seen or heard; things that have not even entered our hearts.

1 Corinthians 2:9 (ESV)
But, as it is written, "What no eye has seen,
nor ear heard, nor the heart of man imagined,
what God has prepared for
those who love him"—

The Gospel writings are packed with supernatural things that confirm that you and I are extraordinary. Let's look at what the physician Luke had to say on one occasion about our extraordinary God.

Luke 8:24-25 (ESV)
And they went and woke him, saying, "Master,
master, we are perishing!" And he awoke
and rebuked the wind and the raging waves,
and they ceased, and there was a calm.
He said to them, "Where is your faith?"
And they were afraid, and they marveled,
saying to one another,

"Who then is this, that he commands even
winds and water, and they obey him?"

This text emphasizes how extraordinary Jesus was. Jesus asked them, *"Where is your faith,"* as if they could and should have done that extraordinary act themselves and without awakening him. In this scripture, Jesus is telling us that we are called to do extraordinary things, just as Jesus Himself during His earthly walk. I'm excited just to know that I'm called to do extraordinary things. John had some things to say about greatness, also:

John 14:12 (ESV)
"Truly, truly, I say to you, whoever believes
in me will also do the works that I do; and
greater works than these will he do, because
I am going to the Father.

When the writer says, *"greater works than these will we do,"* we know that God is expecting us to do not just great things, but extraordinary things. Here's a though, Jesus walked on water and will fly over it?

When I think of extraordinary in the world today, lots of women come to mind; like my mother rearing 9 kids and a host of grandchildren with little money and little help. One of the things she did that was extraordinary was show the older children things so that they could teach the younger ones. That's how we made progress and survived. We looked out for one another until the babies were able to fend for themselves. This strategy was ingenious on my mother's part, we had nothing and lack nothing. It's hard to win today because people are always looking for dirt, so when a brother or sister keeps their name clean we must celebrate them right away. Look at some of the most influential people today. Two women come to mind. I'm sure there's many, many more, but two for now. *Oprah Winfrey,* and the incomparable *Michelle Obama.* Oh, just to say their names is a breath of fresh air. Trust me on this ladies, *class never goes on notices…* When you look up class and integrity in the dictionary, Oprah would be on one page and Michelle would be on the other and both will refer to extraordinary and then back to each other; not just because of the money or fame, but for the way they carry themselves along the way of life *(zero scandals)*. Extraordinary on steroids.

My mother would always say, *"It's not where you come from, but where you want to go in life."* That's still good today. If you can get people to understand that getting there and staying there are two different things and how you get there means everything...

(My inner thoughts). A good way to know you made it, is when people must lie on you to get dirt on you. They lie because what they have on you is too clean to talk about, like for Mr. Obama. They must dig up dirt and disguise it in trickery to get over on him, or Nelson Mandela, what did he do so... bad to spend #27 years in jail? You and I know people right now in our government between 2016-2020 that should be in jail doing a life sentence, but never people that walk in extraordinary integrity. When that happens, you've made it. When we look at reality TV today it saddens me, because we are living way under the extraordinary lives that God intended for us, some things are good clean fun, but some of the stuff is just plain downright filthy to the point of Enough!!! The things our kids see on TV are scandalous, and we wonder why some men stick and move so easy, reality makes it look glamorous. Some of us change woman like we change underwear and leave are ladies flat, I for one don't agree with that mindset!

You must remember that Hollywood are actors acting. That's not real life, it's their job. What we see on TV is ordinary, fabricated with falsehood, it's called acting. This is who you are!

1 Peter 2:9 (ESV)
But you are a chosen race, a
royal priesthood, a holy nation, a people for
his own possession, that you may proclaim
the excellencies of him who called you out of
darkness into his marvelous light.

"Marvelous light" is an extraordinary concept! Remember we were once in darkness, slavery, and bondage, but God called us to a higher place in him and that's Extraordinary. The women in the Bible I've mentioned all have one thing in common, and that's a core value to make things right. For instance, Ruth and Naomi had loyalty, love and covenant, genuine love that keeps its promises, even in broken places. Rahab had her faults -- lying and hiding the spies and being a prostitute, which was not glamorous work -- but she had something many don't; and that was her love for God. David was just wrong in his pursuit of Bathsheba, but his love for God overshadowed the sin. As for Mary, she was the mother of love -- extraordinary love. She carried all power -- Jesus! If she carried that type of power one can only imagine what type of power she has left in her.

Women have traveled many paths to be extraordinary, and despite being treated as little more than slaves sometimes, have still managed to come out victoriously. Now that's extraordinary. Elizabeth said something to Mary that all women need to say to one another: *"Blessed are you among women and blessed is the fruit of your womb."* Even when you're down and out your body is producing blessings.

Elizabeth and Mary had to question why God granted them a role in his great plan, because they knew

God owed them nothing. But they also knew that God had given them much.

As Luke 12:48 affirms, *"Everyone to whom much was given, of him much will be required.*

Sarah could do nothing but laugh after hearing God's proclamation to her husband. She could have cried, but extraordinary people don't quit; they adjust. And that's just what these women did in their unique circumstances -- *old, barren, virgin, widow, liar....* You name it; each woman overcame her challenges to be extraordinary. Ladies, you must keep moving forward and don't ever let *anything or anybody* stop you from being Extraordinary you.

Chapter 10

What Am I Worth?

One of the hardest questions that people ask themselves is, *am I good enough?* In almost every walk of life. For certain, we shouldn't have to question our own worthiness, but sometimes we are overly critical of ourselves... A dog is called man's best friend in the eyes of the world. I never read that in the Bible. Jesus is the one who sticks closer than a brother; then your wife is your helpmeet and friend? ...and what about your brothers and sisters? --a dog is out front in man's eyes. That's what the world says. I can see why people go around trying or looking for acceptance in people and things; *but still believe they are never good enough.* Some groups make it clear that if others don't have this or that, they're not good enough to qualify for membership. (High society).

After all we go through -- all the hurts and pain, the ups and downs, doors opened and shut in our faces -- you would think that when you get to the forgiven church, all of your insecurities and fears would go away. Unfortunately, no; the human side of the forgiven church is just another starting place to feel all of what you felt in the world. So, I ask myself, "What am I worth?"

You know, it's really easy to understand unsaved people giving you the cold shoulder, but the church should have a warm place of welcome for everyone just because of the love God has for them. When I think about where God brought me from, I can't help but have a warm and loving spot for other people. Marvin Sapp sang a song called *"Never Would Have Made It."* That song is my testimony, because when I think about where I was and where I'm now, it was no body but God that brought me out of the dark places I ones live in. So now, having been set free from sin by the master of the universe, to be wondering about my worth is an insult to my God. It was God who brought you and me out of darkness into His marvelous light. So, today my answer to you when it comes to your worth is yes, you're worth it all: all the love and kindness God has to give.

If God had not found you to be worthy, you never would've made it to where you are now. Many people may wonder, *"What if I stopped coming around?* Would they even notice I was gone?"* Insecurity alone can cause you to lose confidence about yourself and your ability to do things well. This book, Penalties for Not Being A Lady First is critical to your success if you're ever going to get the respect you so rightfully deserve. You need to know your worth, and he must know your value: your usefulness and importance. I'm talking to the ladies because you make things and people better. You're very important and significant in God's eyes – the most important eyes in the universe. In other words, there's no me without you...

How much am I worth should never be your question, but if you find yourself asking it, the answer is *(everything).* That's right! That's my message to the ladies all over the world, and people in general. You have great value. If you only know one scripture make sure it is this one:

1 John 4:17 (ESV)
By this is love perfected with us, so that we
may have confidence for the day of judgment,
because as he is so also are we in this world.

This scripture tells of your greatness -- *"As He is, so are we"* – which confirms that you are great. Whether it's baking cookies or keeping home and family together, you make it better. I can remember growing up as a kid, going outside to play ashy, dry and dirty my mother would wipe my face with spittle in her hands or the hem of her dress to clean me up like a pet. She would lick, spit, and wipe me off I would look smooth and clean. I was smelling better and looking good also I don't know what happened, but I did felt better. If we just knew our value, our lives would be so much easier. Please don't spit on me today, I'd rather use the sink and a washcloth, but that's what moms did to make you better sometimes outside on the run.

According to a recent article in *Wired magazine*, a body could be worth up to $45 million dollars, a figure derived from calculating the prices for bone marrow, DNA, lungs, kidneys, and hearts as separate components. That's the world study, and sometimes the world can sell you cheap. A hundred years ago, Dr. Charles H. Mayo, then president of the American Medical Association wrote an article entitled, *"Our Bodies' Worth"* in which he stated that a human body was only worth $0.84. Research today reveals that the basic worth of the elements of an individual human body is $4.50: $3.50 for the skin, and $1.00 for the remaining body parts. Almost a hundred years have passed and the increase in value is only $ 3.66 from Dr. Mayo's long-ago calculation. We can't say that we have increased in market value, but at least we aren't worth any less. A quote attributed to Thomas Edison said that from a man's neck down he is worth a couple of dollars a day, but from his neck up, he is worth anything that his brain can produce. That sounds better than Dr. Mayo's calculation, but it still does not measure up to the value God places on each of us. This is Gods idea of us.

Psalm 8:4 (ESV)
What is man that you are mindful of him,
and the son of man that you care for him?

God gave up his only son and it wasn't for money. He did it for love and abundant life -- today and for eternity. **God is mindful of us.** In other words, we never leave His mind. How man can put a value on human life is beyond me. People should never be valued in dollars and cents. To do so is *"prehistoric, even barbaric"* in my option. God values you and me at a much higher price-- His Son's life. Now how do you price that? It's like saying to a woman, how much is your child worth? There is no number. Well, that's just how God sees us: we are priceless. Your value is far beyond a price tag; that's how much you're worth to God. In fact, David the psalmist asked a loaded question: *"What is man that you are mindful of him?"* David asked the question mainly because everything God created He gave it to you and to me-- for all of mankind. God is so mindful of us that He gave us the world in the form of

His only Son, as payment for our sins. And as a bonus, He throw in the earth.

Psalm 115:16 (ESV)
The heavens are the Lord's heavens,
but the earth he has given to the
children of man.

The question remains, *"What is man?"* David was so in awe and splendor of creation and the wonder of nature that it led him to praise the Creator; even the universe with its infinite distance was the work of the Lord's fingers. He was not only in tune, but focused. Creation was fine, but the Creator was divine and everything He had He gave it to man. Now think about your value. Where do you start? How do you put a price on someone who owns everything? What are we worth? As I stated earlier, the answer is Everything. Therefore, you need to know what God says about you, not man. Ladies, one of the things we all must do is not only to ask, *"what am I worth?"* but also to ask, *who am I?* and *to whom do I belong?* The answer is God, who created you in His image and exact likeness. If somebody can tell me what God is worth, then maybe we can find a price for you and me.

Ladies, there are three powerful words to consider in life. I call them the three **Cs:** *choice, chance,* **and** *change.* You must make a choice to take a chance or your life will never change. One of the worst things you can do as a lady is lose your identity. Making bad relationship choices with men is one of the ways that you forfeit the chance to change for the better. If you asked ten women their biggest mistake in relationships with men, nine out of ten of those women would tell you that their biggest mistake was moving in with them out of wedlock or sleeping with them too soon. Because God made you in His image, second best is not an option for you. If He doesn't think enough of you to marry you, then he's not thinking about you. *How you doing? In my Wendy Williams voice.* In the vastness of creation, God thought a lot about you all the way down to saving the best for last, (you). Male and female stand at the summit of God's creation, but female was arguably his **secret sauce.** Male and female were created at the same time, but the woman was kept hidden under cover in Adam's side for a pacific time.

Genesis 1:27 (ESV)
So, God created man in his own image,
in the image of God he created him;
male and female he created them.

Genesis 2:21 ESV)
So, the Lord God caused a deep sleep to fall
upon the man, and while he slept took one of
his ribs and closed up its place with flesh.

He could have gone back to the ground to make the woman, but no He used Adam's rib to symbolize the place where we are supposed to keep our ladies; covered and close, not under our feet, where we keep the devil. God designed the woman as the man's helpmeet to hold men together; therefore, God's creation was intentional. That's how much you are worth.

I follow sports a little and two sports come to mind when I think about women: baseball and basketball.

One has a six man, and the other has a clean-up man, or person. In basketball the sixth man doesn't start the game but is very valuable to the team's success. His job is to come in when one of the starters gets winded or needs further instructions to strategize how to win the game. He's not only coming in to relieve the winded player, but he sees what you couldn't see while you were running up and down the floor or field. He comes in and takes advantage of the player's weakness for the win, because he has fresh legs and lots of energy. Although he's not a starter he helps the team win the game. *Hang on I'm going somewhere...* The clean-up man in baseball lets and hope all the batters before him get on base. His job is to hopefully hit the ball far enough, so all the players run the bases and make it to home plate for the win, even if he gets out. The woman God made for man is are six man and clean up person, sort of speak. She and she alone help us win in every area of our lives. *--oh, and one more thing...* they both sit the bench waiting for the opportunity to shine, or should I say help out not caring if they get out, but for the team to win. *MJ is bad, but she's bad-der... Hee - Hee...in my Michael Jackson voice...*

She was hidden in Adam for God's glory. She sees exactly what man needs, though she is undercover, because she was with man all the time. That sounds just like The Master, who said, *"I will never leave you or forsake you."* You can't see God, but He's right there with you all the time helping you to win in every area of life. Sometimes, the people who help you the most are not out front. Sometimes, they're behind the scenes getting things done. Lots of our ladies are behind the scenes, so when we talk about worth remember, she's priceless. If you don't believe me, look at most great men and hear their testimonies. One of the first people they will talk about is their wives. Sometimes she single handedly saves the whole household. That's what Rahab did.

Joshua 2:12 (ESV)
Now then, please swear to me by
the Lord that, as I have dealt kindly with you,
you also will deal kindly with my father's
house, and give me a sure sign

Rahab was very valuable. Her one act, though it was a lie, saved her whole family. The Creator said it best, *"It's not good for man to be alone."*

Genesis 2:18 (ESV)
Then the Lord God said, "It is not good that
the man should be alone; I will make him a
helper fit for him."

He made woman for man, not man for woman. Talk about special... This is where her worth comes in. God actually took a rest after creating the heavens and the earth, and the beast of the grounds, then formed woman. And on the seventh day He rested. He made woman and brought her to man. When we talk about worth, this is the kicker, He formed -- arranged or planned in a particular way – the man. That's nice, but when you make something, you build and shape it in a specific way, to your own specifications; like a potter. If the potter's creation is not to his specifications, he starts all over again. God made you clearly and exactly with his own hands and specifications. The man was formed in the image of the Father, Son, and the Holy Spirit.

Genesis 1:26 (ESV)
Then God said, "Let us make man] in our
image, after our likeness.

Then God organized the Trinity, one Godhead. Like an assembly line work (sort to speak), that's the type of work people do every day. He manufactured man. His creation was good, but arguably, the apex in creation had to be the woman. God said, *"Let us make man in our image, after our likeness"* in Genesis 1:26, without particular specifications, He had help making man. He could have had made two men in creation saying that! Will actually He did, *(wo-man and man)* one had a womb to bring life, but that's a whole nother story. Anyway, God rested and put great thought into making the woman with His own hands, *(one on one)*. That's what you're worth. When you know you want to do something great, you first get some rest and count the cost.

Luke 14:28 (ESV)
For which of you, desiring to build a tower,
does not first sit down and count the cost,
whether he has enough to complete it?

Well, that's just what God did for the woman, He counted the cost. Now you should be starting to see your worth, regardless of what Dr. Charles Mayo calculated about our body's worth or what society says. You cost more than a *McRib sandwich (man's rib)*. The place He made you from says a lot about you and your significance.

(To reiterate) God did not bring you from the head, back, or feet, but from the side. If He made you from the head, you would rule over man; from the back, you would always be walking behind man; from the feet, you would be under man. But no; He made you from the man's side, so that you would, always walk together with man in dominion and power. That's why touching and agreeing is so powerful: when two people are on the same page, nothing can stop them.

Matthew 18:19 (ESV)
*Again, I say to you, if two of you agree on
earth about anything they ask, it will be done
for them by my Father in heaven.*

Ladies get to know your worth. I'm not going to hold the past against you, because if you don't know much, you can't do much. That's water under the bridge; but now that you know, the clock starts ticking. When God made you, He counted the cost and finished. That alone is a lot to thank God for, because God is a finisher even on the cross. With His last breath, will and testament in one He proclaimed, *"it is finished"* and that completion includes you! Instead of asking "How much am I worth?" we should be asking God, *"What do I owe you, for dying on the cross for me?"* Nothing, even though the price He paid for your worth, was His life for your life. Because you are worth Everything to Him.

When God created Adam, He was finished, but not complete, so He made the woman, Eve, from the rib. God knew just what He needed from and for Adam to complete all his work: an open womb. He opened Adam and closed him back. What an architect! But God left

Adam's leading lady open so that she could bring life and finish His work. Are you starting to see your value yet? Simply stated, there is no man without woman. The world would cease to exist without you! That's huge.

Adam and Eve were supposed to be fruitful and multiply on this earth but failed to do so. Because God is a finisher, He gave the assignment to Noah and his family, because it was God's command in the beginning to be fruitful and multiply.

There's humor in the ribs story...

Adam said to God, "I want a woman who listens to everything I say, cooks and cleans after me, watches TV and sports with me and cheers for the same team I cheer for... that's the type of woman I want... and one more thing, never ever talk back except for *"yes sir" and "no sir"* ...and God said how about a Rib? Lol... Now, you see why I don't do stand-up?

Ladies, you're not just a rib sandwich. FYI, the rib cage holds the upper part of the body together as well as the head, because the spine and the rib cage connect; it supports the neck and holds the head in place... ***Now let's talk about worth again...*** You are the original rib that was made into a woman and who keeps the head from falling to the ground. That must be worth something. Oh, there you go again, holding men together. ***What am I worth*** you ask? Let's give God some praise for a moment. How many people do you know who can turn a rib to a woman? Selah (pause). I know people who can turn meat to bones, but bones to a woman, ***Forget about it.*** When she and we understand her significance and worth, and where she comes from and why -- as a secret agent to help you -- her value will increase just like a diamond after it's free of flaws. She is a precious stone, just like the diamond that always had value; you just couldn't see its worth, but it was always there.

Ladies, your biggest job today is to get rid of the junk in your lives, the deadweights and flaws, so that not only you can see your greatness, but others as well and get back on the high end of life, and live on top of the world. Now that you know your worth, get busy getting your stuff back. As you can see, we can go on and on about your worth, but none of it will matter if you don't display it in the right way -- *display not show off* -- all your personal goods. When you display something, you show things that people can see, just look no touching. But the quality attracts interest. Anytime when there is interest, commitment or loyalty will automatically come. Whenever a person shows interest in something like a car or a house, the first thing he or she is attracted to is the outside. If the outside seems promising, then and only then will the person make a commitment to the inside. ... Understand that just because he sees the inside, he doesn't get to stay there. When you are looking at a house, you just look at the nice furniture and the rooms and see how nice the house is and imagine it as a beautiful place to raise a family. You don't go in and run around and jump up and down on the beds... you just look and say how nice it is. A man can sample food and test drive cars, but never your assets! They are not to be test driven or sampled. Hello...

Ladies save your best for last, like Jesus with the wine: He saved the best for last. Show him who and what you're about, not what you can do with your body parts. Trust me on this, he will love you for it later if you show your value instead of your valuables... If you are asking how to do that without going all the way (good point), remember that going all the way is so juvenile today. If you don't believe me ask your girlfriend that got involved to soon with Mr. wrong. When a real player sees your value, he doesn't want to play anymore because most men really want families; a little junior to brag about who will carry his name. Trust me, most men stop looking for true relationship when the value goes down and that goes for almost everything; whether it is physical value or material value, you're not paying top price for a used anything, are you? Keeping your panties up until the right time will stop your value from going down like the Titanic. ***What I just gave you deserves an encore; standing ovation.***

Let me tell you an analogy about fishing. If fishermen are ever going to catch good sized quality fish, they first must have good, juicy bait. The same goes with relationships. Nobody want to be in a humdrum, dull relationship; so, used the good stuff your qualities. Remember, Jesus saved the good wine for last. Never give up the goods too fast. You put good quality out front on the hook you'll get good returns -- the big fish. That strategy works in business and in every part of life. If a farmer puts good seeds in the ground, he will get a good harvest, if normal conditions are right -- you know, sun, rain, good fertilized ground -- that's just the way it works. Look at most great athletes, we never see the hard work that was put in until game night, the seeds that was planted show up in front of Millions to enjoy.

Ladies bait your hook not always to catch, but to attract. Then you can pick what you want from the catch once it's on board -- think of it as a good big catch. If you ever watch the History channel or the Explorer channel, you know that the fishermen sometimes throw out good bait just to attract a better variety of fish. That's a lesson in itself, but the point I want to bring home is, ladies, never stop putting your best foot forward (again), because you only get one time to make a *first impression*. Truthfully, most men want a woman they can trust. It's a lonely world if he can't trust you, but he will invest in you to the tune of houses, cars, everything he owns, and loyalty if he can trust you. If you think about your last failed relationship, distrust was probably present and a major reason it ended. Trust is a lonely word. Whoever brings trust into a relationship will automatically win, even if he or she is a jerk. Trust stands alone, It's a drawing card. Everybody wants it like money but can get but so much of it.

Your worth is more precious than life itself. Did you know that the money that men voluntarily give to women with no judge, court or jury it's Billions of dollars? Tap into your worth, and stop getting paid like Dumbo the circus elephant, who was working for peanuts. Get back to Eden and live on top of the world.

God made us just a little lower than the angels, and crowned us with His glory. In other words, praise, power, honor, fame, and -- oh yes – money lots of it, is supposed to be huge parts of our lives. We are majestic creatures who are to rule over creation. In our fallen state, we are profoundly disfigured by sin; however, He restored those who put their trust in Him. There is that word *"trust"* again, it's the glue in relationships.

In Christ, we recover all; in Him, we move, live and have our being we become the people God wanted us to be. So, whenever you're feeling worthless, the word of the psalms should encourage you. We are valuable people because God Himself created us in His image likeness, (exactly like Him). Think about that: when we talk about the worth of women, or people in general we are talking about God's glory.

When you talk or think about your worth, just remember God gave it all just for you and me: He gave His son Jesus, the Christ, that is what you're worth. Everybody is trying to understand or make the comparison between angels and humans. That's where God placed us. When a woman chooses not to be a lady first, she complicates things with that decision. Not because she's so bad, but the mindset of man is so warped when it comes to woman and her place in life. A man's sins are so easily forgiven by others in the world, but a woman's sins follow her to the grave and beyond. Remember the adulterous woman? There was no reason for her sins to follow her so long. All I know is her worth must be very high to the thought of her being human and letting her hair down, so to speak, is beneath her worth. Isn't it ironic that God allowed Adam to name everything on earth except the woman? God was the first to call you woman. That means that you are of great worth to Him.

Genesis 2:22 (ESV)
And the rib that the Lord God had taken from the man he made into a woman and brought her to the man.

God trusted Adam to name almost everything on earth, but when it came to woman, He wasn't leaving the woman to chance. Adam had not failed yet with Eve's name, but God stepped in just in case, so that Adam wouldn't name her wrong. That's how much the woman is worth. God Himself named you. *Boy that's something to shout about all by itself.* The woman God made had more work to do, so He cared for the woman Himself in advance, knowing she would one day care for and carry Him. On one occasion it was Mary, the sister of Martha, the brother of Lazarus who anointed Jesus' feet and used her hair as a towel to dry his feet. This Mary understood her worth. The costly oil she used to anoint Jesus was worth three hundred denarii. One denarius was a laborer's wage for one day. Thank God for the woman, because most men would have let Jesus die stinking. That's the worth of a woman, along with her intuition knowing Jesus was coming back, she didn't want him smelling bad saving souls, so she prepared the body. She anointed the man who would one day heal her as well as mankind. The Bible went on to say that wherever this gospel is preached in the whole world, what this woman had done will be a memorial to her. That's bigger then the *(Heisman trophy award or any Championship)* recognition you can get on earth, it always has value.

Ladies, there is a price on your head and it's costly. All throughout the gospels and in the canons of faith, this woman's worth will be celebrated. She was there in the beginning and in the end at the cross. It was the woman working overtime proving her worth in advance. When we look at what this woman did for Jesus in His time of need, her faith was simply amazing. She showed her worth by helping and comforting him. She just did what she was made to do -- help -- and because of that, her name is synonymous with the gospel. What can be bigger then what she did for Jesus, to carry, birth and to prepare for death while being there when he rose again? That must be worth something.

Knowing your worth means you don't have to turn tricks for any man. All you have to do is glean like Ruth, and watch a good man find you. You will then be living on top of the world. That may sound easy or simple, but that is what you were made to do: be a help meet, not someone's personal whore or prostitute. When you do things that are unbecoming of a lady, your worth stays the same in God's eyes, but your value goes way down with the men. That's where the imbalance comes in. That's why God had to name you, because man would have changed your name and lost the meaning of *w-o-m-a-n*. Your worth could have been jeopardized, but God cemented your worth. But you have to keep up your value. Like a house, you're responsible for the upkeep -- you know – the regular maintenance. When Adam failed, God used Noah and his family to fill the earth, but He never replaced the woman with or for anyone. In other words, no one can take your place. You are the cat's meow, and the vessel to bring life.

Leviticus 18:22 (ESV)
You shall not lie with a male as with a woman; it is an abomination.

This is a hard topic to talk about, but because my job is helping people we must talk. This is for all believers, if you are not a believer of the word of God this may not apply to you! According to this text; Any other lifestyle is a curse; an abomination concerning the legitimacy with same-sex, remember that you are fearfully and wonderfully made by God's hands. God made Adam for Eve. If friends don't let friends drink and drive, Christians shouldn't let friends live in sin we all sin and fall short of God's glory. Just like God made woman for man He also made woman to bring life. Ladies, men see your worth and try to get with you once he conquered a man may have realized just how much you're worth, but you served it wrong. Think about serving a thick, juicy steak, baked potato, butter, sour cream, and chives on a dirty garbage lid. Now he wants a steak, *but not that one.* The steak is good, but it lost its value by being served on a garbage lid instead of a nice, clean plate. That is what is happening every day to women who do not know where to draw the line about serving their goods the wrong way. You were made to help, not to be someone's love slave.

This next text: is an awesome story; about a woman looking for love in all the wrong places.

John 4:16-17 (ESV)
Jesus said to her, "Go, call your husband, and
come here." The woman answered him,
"I have no husband." Jesus said to her,
"You are right in saying, 'I have no husband';

The Samaritan woman had five husbands, and immediately, her value went down because she had given herself away to different men. The adulterous woman had a similar situation. Her value went down, but Jesus sealed her worth, by forgiving her sins and encaged her heart, some of the towns people wanted her stone, and as they continued to ask Him about her sins, He stood up.

John 8:7 (ESV)
And as they continued to ask him,
he stood up and said to them, "Let him who is
without sin among you be the first to
throw a stone at her."

Ladies, your worth can never be replaced. You must hold on to it and hold on even tighter to your value because your value is the thing that gets you to the next level in life. Many people on top got there on a good recommendation, but your value will get you there faster and longer every time. One of the quickest ways to lose your value is to live beneath your potential. Most people invest in other people more than themselves. That's a sure way to lose your value. If any guy thinks enough to sleep with you, you need to help his thinking, and think your way to a good marriage counselor. That's a good scare tactic, so that you see where he's coming from.

Not trying to throw off on the men, but if he's serious about you he'll make the appointment with the pastor … Let's keep it one hundred, sex mess a lot of good people up! Can I get an amen?

Women have been saving lives since the beginning of time, thus proving their worth. One of the greatest saves was me, ***when God saved me from my very worst enemy, when He saved me from myself…***

True story…

My wife married me on credit. The long and short of the story was before we met I was on my way to the ATL…

that's right *hot Atlanta* to live. I was purposely going to work three jobs for fun. I had a plan, or so I thought. I was going to be a hairdresser by day, bartender by night, and a male dancer on the weekends. My dancing name was going to be **Chocolate Thunder,** (smile)... Real talk. I was going to shave my head bald, get hazel contacts, get tatted up, and hit the gym hard... you know for bigger muscles. Before going, it was told to me dancers make good money on the weekends showing off their muscular bodies. My wife now was my girlfriend then she called me at that time, we had pagers, not cell phones. I was on I-95 south doing about 85mph, and my beeper went off, it was my future wife if she had not called, I was out in Hot Atlanta. I was done with being faithful in relationships. Honesty was a lonely word and I was done with being exclusive with one woman girlfriends became a joke, because honesty was a lonely word. Then God sent me a woman worthy to love. Not to put my wife on the top shelf, put remember, earlier I said whoever brings trust into the relationship wins. Well, that's just what happened, she brought trust. Trust opened me up to be committed to one person and my heart led the way to true love.

I don't know how much I was in love with her, but I knew I was not interested in having just a sex partner. I was done with that! As far as I was concerned, I was not committing to sex with just one woman when I could get that *anywhere* **and** *almost anytime.* But I stopped being a player that day, cold turkey, and a year later, I asked for her hand in marriage. We've been married 20 years and counting... I was done with broken-down, no value, worthless relationships. I refused to invest in another woman just to have sex. I was going to have it on my terms, with no strings attached. That's what happens when your value goes down; men lose heart. The heart still works; but it has no feelings for love –or should I say true love. That is one of the major penalties for not being a lady first, giving yourself away for free. The man replaces *(love with lust.)* The only thing those words have in common is that they both start with *(L)*.

Ladies, going forward make sure the (L) is followed with (O-V-E) and not, (U-S-T). Some guys will give you all the attention you want until you give it up -- you know what! *do the nasty* -- but then lose respect for you. He begs you until you do, but when you do he buggs out! *Talk about a strange bird.* Whatever you do ladies, going forward, don't trade your value for a (screw.) Make sure that when you do, he has the right letters in the right place after that (L), because it's a matter of life and death, mainly for you. Remember this: you have amazing power. You once carried the King of kings and Lord of lords and He has all power. Whether you know it or not, most men are already sold on you; that's why we're always running behind you. Wake up! All you have to do is seal the deal. You already have him! Always remember: Sex is your equalizer, not your weapon. Stop killing your chances for (real love) with loose, illicit sex showing all you're *a-s-s-e-t-s.* Put your stuff away and show your worth. Remember, you have amazing power.

Story time...

I was watching *The Wiz,* with Diana Ross, Michael Jackson *(my cousin, LOL) ... *remember when Michael was everybody's cousin?*

'Diana, who played Dorothy in *The Wiz*, had all the power inside of her. The wizard, played by Richard Pryor, disappointed Dorothy, the Scarecrow, and the Tin Man, followed by the Cowardly Lion. The characters in the play, including Dorothy, were originally looking for the wizard to show them the way home. When the wizard's balloon flew away, it was Dorothy who took leadership and showed them the *yellow brick road*. In the beginning of the movie, the (good witch) showed them a way out and said, *"If you want the things that are missing in your life and make it home, follow the yellow brick road."* Ladies, you have been helping people for a long time, from the inside out, and you had the power in you all the time. It was the woman who once again came through and showed them the way. It is because you know more about us than we know about ourselves. Remember, while Adam was exploring earth and naming all the animals, the woman on the other hand, was inside of man disguised as a rib exploring his insides and learning all about him. In this story ironically all the characters walking the yellow brick road were men, that is saying something, because Dorothy was the lead out of all the men including the Wiz.

Ladies I rest my case. You are worthy of all the praise. That's what you are worth: everything. That's why God gave you His Son to carry, knowing He would arrive safely. He knew up front you knew the way out, so the Son gave His life. Ladies, you are not only worthy; you are the cream of the crop. When a man says he loves you going forward, say back to him, *"You should put a ring on it."* Then show him the yellow brick road to how much you are worth, with increase and save your value, and maybe his life. That's what you're worth… still

want to know what your worth? ...let me tell you again
Everything!!!

Chapter 11

Forty-One, Trying to Find
My Thirty-One

Out of all the chapters in this book, this one has to be the reason for writing. I watch women from all over the world take a beating on Tv, or in the movies or unfortunately in real life. Some women's whole lives consist of trying to please a man or other people. For some reason, she comes up short every time. I have four sisters, a host of nieces, and a mother, so you can see my investment in this issue. I believe men have confused the hell out of women about what they want and need. Now she has no idea about what he is looking for in a woman. From the beginning of time, women have been supporting us men, all the way from *(Main Street to Wall Street)*. With all that support, you would think that she, of all people, would have the best seat in the house concerning relationships with men, but not so. She still gets the rough end of almost every deal, from marriage to business and all in between. *Lord, send the help... for our ladies.*

With the help she has given us, I think it's only fair that we men salute her. *That's right.* Ladies, you need to know that without you, our world would be a (Gigantic landfill), and instead of waste material being burned, it would be us men. I don't know if that makes you feel any better about yourself, but it is the truth. Most of us would be sick with the thought of losing you, but for some crazy reason, we won't tell you that. Well now I'm speaking for all men, hopefully: we not only love and adore you, we would be like a ship without a sail in the middle of the ocean without you. A ship without a sail is going nowhere! Without you, we would be just drifting away.

Now that you've heard the truth about us, and the way most men feel about you, I believe things will get better for you in future relationships. There's a place in life that women must get to It is a place that most, if not all men have been looking for you all the time; and some, not all have never visited that place, let alone stayed.

I was in a conversation one day with my wife, just about life and people she talks with in general. And out of nowhere, she said something that shocked me to writing. Evidently it was something beneath her, and she said, *"I don't have time for that type of conversation, if it's negative."* Then later she said to me, "Honey, I'm 41 trying to find my 31." *Well, great balls of fire!* That' conversation is why I wrote this chapter. Can you believe that all I asked her was, "why do you keep dealing with girlfriends that come and go in your friendship" Will I think she had enough?

That's it ladies, the place, the secret you've been trying to find forever is right in front of you. You've looked everywhere high and low, you've done everything trying to please a man and what you were looking for eluded you... but now I found the *genie in the bottle.* Yes, a genie; just like the one in stories and movies. A magic spirit that looks like a person that lives in the lamp, or bottle and serves the person who calls it out. You know the (fairy tale). If you didn't hear anything I just said, hear this... (A genie must serve the person who calls it out). That's the place ladies you must get to and I have the magic potion. Actually, it's not magic; it's in the Word of God, Proverbs 31, to be exact. The subject of that chapter is called the *"Proverbs 31 woman, or the virtuous woman"*. If you ladies ever find this place, all your heartaches and disappointments will disappear. Most of women's heartaches, I believe, come from bad relationships with men anyway, that's what my wife thinks, not bills.

Don't put your dogs on me, I'm just the mailman.

I'm an ex-ball player and Golden Gloves champ. One of the things I liked when I played was that teams had to be evenly matched, so we'd have good games. If there was no real competition, to me, it was no fun. Beating easy opponents or smaller guys was boring to me. I always like beating the best, the bigger, the stronger, and the faster; that's the game for me. One of the guys I played ball with said to me one day, "You're really good! How old are you?" I said, "54." He said, "You're still the best out here and the oldest." I said, "That's because I like playing and beating the best, It's a challenge to me they keep me in shape and on my toes." With that said, it's only fair to give our ladies the right information about what men are looking for so the teams will be evenly matched, and the ladies can compete and start winning, or at least put up a good fighting pursuit of lasting relationships. And we can have good games, (relationships). *Now, if you're ready let's go.*

One of the main thing's men are looking for in a woman is someone who is morally good. TA-DA! That's it! It's not your money or your honey, even though both are good I might add... If a guy is serious about you, all he's really looking for is to see what your characteristics are like, what kind of morals you have and where you draw the line as to what you will or will not do. (Trust me; that is huge for us). We want you to do everything for us sexually only, that's why you must keep that genie in the bottle, so to speak. Why do you think some guys can have sex with you and leave you like it never happened? Because sex is an action, anybody can do that, but character and integrity are parts of a lifestyle. Animals have sex, but having good morals is something only humans have. Animals go around smelling butts and having sex with any other animal of their species in heat. No morals. Most men, like the genie in the bottle, were created to serve and care for the one who calls it out. His woman.

Ladies stop over-shooting and giving yourself away. Your goal in relationships, ladies, is to call him out so he can serve you. He's already turned on by you. All you must do now is *call him out*. When I say call him out, I mean show him what he's missing by not having you as his leading lady. We've seen big butts and breasts, but one thing most men have not seen much of is a **Lady** ... I don't know if you're ready, but this is the big one.

Ephesians 5:25 (ESV)
Husbands love your wives, as Christ loved the church and gave himself up for her,

Husbands love your wives. Husbands are to emulate Christ: just like Christ laid down his life for the church, husbands are supposed to do the same. No one must die for the church anymore; Christ did that already. Men are to serve their wives to the point of suffering. Ladies, the only laying down that you should be doing is for your husband, so he can serve you. Hello... *Ladies, can I get an amen?* Believe it or not, ladies, you've got the genie in the bottle, and I know you know where it's at, right, right.... He's just waiting to be called out. That's the 41 finding her 31. A Proverbs 31 woman knows how to call him out and not just verbally. He's been looking all over for you -- that special one. My wife was 41 years old at the time I started writing this book that's where the title of this chapter came from. It doesn't matter what age you are; *just find your 31.* The Bible says, who can find a virtuous wife or woman it's almost like the Bible is saying that she's lost or hard to find; a rarity; not common; or unusual... almost like she doesn't exist. That's what men have been looking for forever since the fall of Adam, because that's what been put into man's hands, you for me. Adam fell and lost you and he's been looking for you ever since. Before the fall, God made you and gave you to Adam and he's been trying to find you again in that God place. When he's with Sue and Jane and she's with John and Luther looking for love in all the wrong places, she's just trying to find her 31, and he's trying to get his 31.

Woman, you must get back to the old landmark: family -- husband, wife, and kids -- so we all can find our way back to oneness with each other. The Bible talks about how this virtuous woman's worth is above rubies. (The hardest stone after Diamonds). Somebody is not getting paid what she's really worth if she's worth so much, why is she getting so little? I think it's because her ability and nobility have great worth. She has ability and special skills to do great things, and her nobility has a quality with high social class. In other words, she's a mover and shaker. But because she's living beneath her potential, she's getting paid a lot less than she's worth.

Listen to what the writer of Proverbs 31:10 says her *"Worth is far above rubies."* Rubies are one of the hardest minerals next to diamonds. *Look where God placed you.* Look how close you are to greatness. Rubies are the rarest and most precious of all jewels. In other words, you've got it going on and nobody told you well shame on them. You're the strongest of all jewels. Stop tripping, crying, and falling apart when he's not what you think or when he leaves you, learn how to say bye two times, (bye-bye) …because you're not on a ruby level. You're far above rubies, so stop stooping to Bo-Bo's level! If you think he's hating in the *transformation,* watch what he does in the *destination.* Ladies you're the bomb.

(That the place God is taking you Girls) ... Ladies you're the bomb. Really like, tick tick BOOM!

First, you're hard. Next, you're the rarest and most precious of all jewels. *That's shouting music to my ears all by itself.* (Can you hear the music?) (Ladies, now I see why the writer said, *"Who can find her?"* That's because you're a rarity. Forty-one finding her 31 must be the greatest thing a woman can ever do for herself at any age. Men aren't looking for just sex we're not that shallow or slow. We can get sex anywhere; you already know that we're looking for that precious stone.

I can remember when I was growing up, some girls that I knew were hard they were fine as wine with rock hard bodies. We would just look wishing to get with her for that bump and grind we wanted them bad, but they weren't budging. Because of that, we wanted them even more.

Ladies never stop being the stone you are *(tender but tuff)*. You are the rarest and most precious of all jewels. I thought I knew my wife, and I do, but her declaration of being 41 looking for her 31 is taking my respect for her to another level. She's now more precious than I knew. *(Let me help the brothers out)*. Your wife, girlfriend, freak-boo is more than you think. She's far above what you can even imagine. Now, I know it's only fair to inform the ladies that when you find that place *(stability, emotionally and mentally healthy)*, you'll be unstoppable. Musician, song writer *(Babyface)* sang that he'd "pay your rent, buy your clothes and food" but, when you find the 31 places, your money won't be any good with him, because he's paying for everything. Babyface was just paying your rent before the 41 found her place as a Proverbs 31 woman. But when she identifies with the power she possesses, every need will be met, and her house and all her clothes will be paid for. *(King crab legs, steak, high end drinks and caviar on the barber every day)*. Ordinary is a good place for ordinary people, but extraordinary is very different from normal, and that's a 41-woman finding her 31. When she enters that place, her man will find new respect for her. Remember earlier I said he's been looking for you since the fall in the garden, it's true. He found Ms. Right and let her go, because he didn't know or understand her value. *He fell in lust and right out.* He took a test drive that allowed him to see just what he was getting. If he only knew her value and she knew her worth, lust would never be a major part of our relationships today. Everybody wants what they paid for, especially when it comes to relationships.

One of the reasons I believe divorce rates are so high in and out of the church is because most people think they're getting one thing only to discover they are getting another, *(A 41 who has yet to find her 31).* After the honeymoon is over, the person you married better be the person you're in love with, because people change; but the Proverbs 31 woman shows her true value. One of the saddest things in life is to get something that had worth when you got it but lost its value afterwards. People don't handle that well, so we divorce, forfeit, and buy again. Someone asked an older couple how they stayed happily married for over 50 years, they said, *"We come from a time when something broke, we didn't throw it away, we fixed it."*

Whether your value is great or small, he should know what he's working with. Finding your 31 all by itself is a virtue. If I could say it in one word to the women of the world it would be, *(find your 31... and never lose it!)* Ladies, you may never know how great you are, but you need to know this; all throughout the scriptures, wisdom is referred to as *"her" or "she,"* implying that the gender of *"wisdom"* is a lady. Let me say this s-l-o-w, so no one gets hurt... If wisdom is a woman, wouldn't you think everybody would need one? The most powerful thing on earth is addressed to the female. Wisdom, Mother Nature, and favor must be the strongest things going today. Listen to what the Word of God says about a wife.

Proverbs 18:22 (ESV)
He who finds a wife finds a good thing
and obtains favor from the Lord.

Everything that pertains to a woman in God's eyes brings life, favor, and wisdom. Could it be that when God said it is not good for man to be alone and made him, woman? Could it be she was the wisdom that gave God the advice all the time in the beginning? (just a thought). It's documented that she is his favor, and she's the main vehicle to life, so I'm convinced that she's the *secret sauce* to our success. When she finds her 31 we'll find our wives and families. A woman's inability to find her 31 is not an excuse for a man to live a loose lifestyle while she is developing. What he's looking for he will find in her. The true nature of man is to leave his mother and father and find his own wife, I feel that when the exchange from parent to finding wife happens, we'll stop the *just friends...* girlfriend with benefits; and maybe she'll stop giving him the combo (you know: *(burger, fries, drink, and shake)*. That's not the way the Proverbs 31 woman should be living. That's a 45 to your head, or two to the body and one to the head, like at the fast food restaurant when you order a number from the menu, and get it all; drink, fries, and a burger. My brothers and sisters, that's not the way life goes. We have enough things breaking down, and families are the last thing we need to fail women giving men the combo is wrong! when she's supposed to be finding her way to becoming a Proverbs 31 woman, the virtuous woman never gives a baller the combo of lick, suck, and stick. That combo is for husbands and wives.

If you lick and suck on me as a girlfriend, that's all you will ever be... a good girlfriend I *really, really enjoy.* **Somebody stop me if I'm lying.** Can we keep it 100? Maybe my number one girlfriend, but never my wife. *(Don't look* *at me like that, I wasn't save all my life)* ... Once you start giving up free milk, it's going to be hard to sell it. You might sell it, but not to the one you've been giving it to for free. (Can I get some help up in here!) ...

Ladies, finding your 31 is very profitable for you. All the time you hear people saying *I have to find myself* well, ladies, I have the perfect place for you to start looking: Proverbs 31. Once you find her, your life will never be the same. What she brings to the table, every man is looking for; and he will entertain all the way to the altar. Start looking for that Proverbs 31 lifestyle of principal, values, excellence and integrity, it's where your Boaz lives. *(Boaz was a wealthy man of God, influential landowner and farmer from Bethlehem).*

Ruth 2:1 (ESV)
Ruth Meets Boaz
Now Naomi had a relative of her husband's,
a worthy man of the clan of Elimelech, whose
name was Boaz.

Boaz ends up marrying a poor Moabite woman. You and I might wonder what this wealthy man would want with this poor woman. It couldn't have been sex, because he's rich, which means he could have gotten sex from any woman at any time so sex was not his reason. He saw what she brought to the table. The most important thing you can bring to any type of interview, from relationships to jobs, is your brain. Nobody wants to see you're sexy when it comes to taking care of his or her million-dollar business, except in the Playboy mansion; and we all know what playboys do with you, right, right. One of the things that stands out to me about Ruth in the face of fear and adversity is she never gave up on Naomi or her God. Too often, people give up on thing to quickly. One of the first steps to finding your Proverbs 31 self is being able to stick and stay, just as Ruth did. She stayed with Naomi in the face of adversity. She stayed faithful, and God was pleased and provided for her.

You might say what's the big deal about staying with her mother-in-law? You know how mother in-law stories go: **always in your business** -- who wants that migraine? In Ruth's case, it wasn't about her mother-in-law, it was about her ability to follow through and stay committed to something she believed in. Ruth went from poor and widowed to married and wealthy all because she found her 31 women. She didn't sleep around with the help, rob, or steal to get to the top. She gleaned in the field, worked hard, and proved her worth. A Proverbs 31 woman is creative and can work with her hands and on her feet (not her back).

If you're ever going to be a contender for any position, you first must put in the work and show up. That's what Ruth did. She used her greatest asset, and it wasn't her charm or beauty, even though she had both. It was her fear of the Lord. I know it sounds simple that's because it is a virtuous woman puts her worth on display and her value goes up. All Ruth did was go to work in the field and God gave her the best of everything. Ladies, you don't have to sleep around to get paid actually, your value goes way down when you do in the scheme of things. All you really have to do is find your 31 and watch the favor of God repay you for your works.

Most women have worked overtime trying to please men from the wrong end of their bodies. Remember this forever, ladies your sex is sacred to a man. It is just for him, for his eyes only if he thinks another man is in the mix! all bets are off for a faithful relationship or future plans. I know you thought that if you give in or put out he would marry you for most men, that kind of woman is not the marrying kind. He wants a saint who won't faint. He begged you forever, I know, been there done that! You gave him what he wanted, or so you thought, and he still didn't come through. Ladies Listen and listen well. Your sex gives you the advantage and how you give it up makes all the difference, when or if it comes to wedding bells.

I must say men are funny. For many of them, when a woman puts out, she's a (hoe), and when she doesn't, she's (stuck up). *Hmmm...* It is best to stay stuck up because you'll have the advantage, for all intent's purposes, protect your worth. If all he wants is sex, you'll know it, but if he wants you, he'll do the work. I'll tell you what the work is later in this chapter.

If ladies just take time to find their purpose in God, their Boaz will find them. The Bible said, *"The man that finds a wife, finds a good thing."* You are that! When a woman shows a man the wrong end of her worth, he likes it, *yep... we do...* but we won't invest in it the right way. Don't ask me why, it is what it is. He's just going to a place where he can get his freak on. *Don't tell the guys I told you that!* It's like going to a strip club and making it rain, *(throwing money at women, in their birthday suit).* Men go and have f-u-n, and even spends lots of money, but after their lap dance and watching you drop it like it's hot, they go home to their wives, where all the bills are paid in full with the benefits package. It's time for women to stop being the UN- Happy Meal in relationships.

Be the *entree* -- the main course of the meal -- and stop selling yourself cheap. The entree is an old-fashioned language in the United States it's accompanied by two small meals; the appetizer and dessert. I liken the order food goes in when dining to how a lady should be received. Before the entree, there's the appetizer. The *appetizer* stimulates the interest if something does not stimulate your interest, you will never be the *main meal.* You see, the appetizer causes your appetite to peak. A real man should stimulate your appetite, or your desire to showcase your value. Don't just show everybody your goods, because when we don't like something we spit it out, and you don't have time for people regurgitating you, or on you.

After the meal is the *dessert,* a sweet food that contains lots of sugars. If the man is not very gentle, sweet, and kind, you will probably never be the main course. *You handle the things you like with care.* Ladies, you have four basic sensations on the tongue called the taste buds (sweet, sour, hot and cool). If your taste buds aren't stimulated in the right way with a guy or your sweet desserts are bitter, *it's not the right guy for you,* and you will never be the entree or main meal; the wife.

A relationship should be the appetizer as you are finding your 31 entrees, because God has so many wonderful gifts in and for women that you can't afford to be a side dish, when God's plan is for you to have and be the whole meal. The entree is the main course, and that you are ladies remember the entree is only one part of the meal. You are supposed to be the appetizer that stimulates, and the main meal that satisfies. The dessert is the sweetness, (melodious) that seals the deal. The only thing coming after that is something to drink to wash it all down. This is what I call a *virtuous meal* --The whole package searched for by a 41 finding her 31. This is a woman's place: a wealthy life in every way. So, stop looking for love in all the wrong places and find your 31.

There are so many great women to talk about who not only feed man but cover them as well. Like my mother, who couldn't feed the family with actual food as the provider, but she fed us wisdom and integrity, and cook the food when Pops brought it in. This is what 41 finding her 31 is all about: helping people move along in life and yourself to move on to bigger and better things. One of the things I'll never forget that my mother taught me was how to help people, because most of us only help people when it's convenient for us. My mother said *"Tony, if you only help people when it's convenient for you, that's not help that's convenience"*. She showed me that a Proverbs 31 move is teaching people how to help other people with no strings attached, because she knew that without her guidance, I would help you only when I found time. *Can I get a witness or a Hello...?* When I think about the Proverbs 31 woman, I think about how every day she tries to win in a losing battle as far as the world system is set up, women get the wrong end of the stick every day. Men get paid more, promoted more often, and recognized more frequently for the same job she does. Needless to say, that's not fair. She's great, extraordinary, wonderful, and blessed, she carries your favor and mine. She puts more in and get less out of this world...and that's bad math. If one and one is two and six and three is nine, if you give me some of yours I'll give you some of mine, so we can all move forward, that's good math. So, let's give the hardest working person alive today -- WOMAN -- her props *(her proper respect)*. You may never get the recognition you so rightly deserve but finding your 31 will put you in a place for him not only to need you even more than he does now, but to honor you as well.

Earlier, I said that I would tell you what *"putting in the work"* means. When we think of work, we think of jobs or activities; things that we do regularly, especially in order to earn money, that is work but the real essence of work is to win at whatever you do. Work is an activity in which one exerts strength to perform something. Ladies, this is it. If he is not regularly exerting strength or energy trying to please or take care of you, he's not on the job and you know what happens when you don't show up to work: you get **fired**. If he can't or won't show you that you are important to him regularly, he's not the one. *That's the work!*

Having a wife, lady, girlfriend or boo is **work**. Ladies, anybody can wine and dine you for a night, but can he dine you when you burned the roast and made gravy to cover it for the third week in a row? That's a whole other dining experience. One of the key things in relationships I said I would never do, is put up with someone for convenience. If he or she can't celebrate you, let him go!

When I started dating my wife, one of the things she used to say to me when I talked freaky to her was, *"I'm not that girl."* It would burn me up. I wanted her, so I put in the work and grew with her in the good and bad times. Now the tables are turned, and she talks freaky to me with her nasty self. Smile... And I say, *"I'm not that guy."* That's because I put in the work, I made a commitment she could trust in, to grow with her in every way. When

I say every way, that's just what I meant and gave her a clear vision of where we were going as a family, that's it.

Ladies and gentlemen, there are going to be times and days in your marriage or relationship that you're going to look at the person you're laying next to and say, *"Who in the hell is this in my bed?"* Your significant other will probably say the same about you also. One time I thought my wife was out to get me; I thought she wanted to hurt me for real -- not my heart, but hurt me physically. When I say grow with her, I mean that sometimes marriage is a roller coaster with a lot of hills, thrills, and thrillers. Sometimes, it's like coming out of a dark tunnel not knowing where you're at going down a hill and your heart drops.

Sometimes a woman doesn't want you to have the answers to life; sometimes she just wants you to listen. Nobody told me that before marriage. I had the answers to everything, so I thought.

One day my wife woke up talking about all that wasn't right in this world she was living in. I thought she was talking about the universe, and all of space, everything in it, including the stars, planets, and galaxies. Boy, was *I* out of touch. I thought, "does she want me to have the answers to the world's problems?" No. All she really wanted to do was tell me about her side of the world she was living in – *Duh* -- not have the answers. I was apologizing for two days because everything I said was wrong. That's marriage, so when is the wedding date again? Lol...

I believe, when a woman finds her 31, her man will find his reason for living. God holds the key to life and death but locked it inside of the woman. That was part of His master plan. Really, you can't move forward without her. *Holy to-le-do Batman!* Everything man needs is locked inside of her. That's right! Your lady holds the key to your life's success. Ladies and gentlemen get this scripture deep in your spirit. Read it on your free time; it applies to him and her. It's a game changer.

2 Corinthians 4:7 (ESV)
But we have this treasure in jars of clay, to show that the surpassing power belongs to God and not to us.

Now can you see why the 31 is so important? There's more inside of your lady than meets the eye and God made her that way, to ensure we who desire the favor of God would find wives. Wow. That's another part of His master plan. Talk about a secret treasure, gentlemen! Think about this: the woman you are trashing is wealthy in every way and holds the success you're looking for inside of her.

Gentlemen, now you know. The woman you're playing with is a walking, talking safe with lots and lots of (bucks) and favor inside of her-- Millions, even Trillions. She needs to find her 31 and you need to find her. What a deal!

The pressure is on both men and women... but since I'm talking to the ladies right now-- sisters find your 31, with or without him, because he'll catch up, and when he does, your value must be associated with great worth. I know it's not fair, but you only get one chance to make a first impression. Guys get chance after chance, for some reason I don't know. So, protect your investments and do yourself a favor and don't come out at night... c-a-u-s-e... *"the freaks come out at night... hut, hut, hut!"* ...and you're not a freak. Remember, the last call in the club when the bar is about to close, and the bartender would say, *"Last call for alcohol."* We would get a drink and do surveillance on the bar like security guards looking for somebody to take home to sleep with. Yes, we did. That's why I said the freaks come out at night. Ladies don't let it be you, because your 31 would never get off the ground.

I think when we as men understands who and what God gave us in the woman, this whole thing would turn around as far as relationships goes. Until we men see the gift in the woman, things will stay the same. If a person gives you a gift and you abuse or mistreat it, you probably won't get another present from that person again. We can rest assured that God is bigger on forgiving, because the woman is the gift given to us men from God, and He's still giving. She must be the most underrated gift ever given to men she was there in the beginning and in the end. When you think about someone like that you should be eager to honor her.

So, why are women having such a hard time finding their 31 and the covering they desire in men? I concluded that when God said, *"It's not good for man to be alone,"* He was telling women in a subliminal way, while she was still the rib part of man, "I'm making you not only for him, but from him." Just like us with God: in Him, we live, move, and have our being she likewise lives, moves, and has her being in man. God Himself made it that way, so we wouldn't be lost and leave each other behind he joined us together from the beginning, what a brilliant mind. Every creature on earth, including plant life, has a seed in it for that seed to grow to bring life, it must connect to its roots. Well, that's where the 41 finding her

31 lives. That's the order God made, not man but God, this place is sacred and ordained by God.

When I think about the little things we do in life, they are simple, but meaningful, like a school having a simple football game. Every year they have something called a homecoming game, where all the present and future alumni come together to celebrate their team's roots as well the growth of the institution. Some celebrate the faculty and staff, keeping in mind we are who we are because of pass alumni. The whole school is in a celebratory state of mind for the whole weekend. That's just a simple ball game at school. If schools understand that staying connected is the way they stay alive and grow, what makes you think we – men and women -- don't have to do the same thing to stay alive?

God has given the Proverbs 31 women not only the goal of finding her 31, but also discovering her roots -- the place she came from: not just her birthplace, but the place God made her from originally -- man. She must find him in good working order, not as a drunk, or pimp, but as the God (lower case g) on this earth. Finding her 31 will help a woman bring a man full circle, to the place where she can be the *virtuous woman* she was made to be and live on top of the world. A woman has a tough job when it comes to making a home and making babies because she is always working against time; taking care of home and family takes lots of time. On top of that, she must juggle bills, camp, before and after school activities. Then, she must transform herself from honey boo-boo lover to soccer mom, even while she's pregnant, and still make sure dinner's on the table. I believe she is worthy of *double honor, if not triple.*

Now, who else can do all of that and still have a life? I think she gets in the most trouble because of time because she needs to bring life into this world and sometimes because of that she makes bad choices in men, doing everything and moving too fast trying to find her place in this life, while her *biological clock is ticking* at the same time. It causes her vision to be blurry sometimes.

One of the most satisfying and exciting things for a woman to do is bring life into this world. If the man comes before she finds her 31, *the carriage will lead the horse;* and we all know that the horse pulls the carriage. I think that's the hold up right there: carriages pulling horses. The horse (the man) is supposed to support and carry the woman. The woman is not supposed to pull the carriage while she cares for the family. Part of her God-given nature is to bring life she can't get away from it, so sometimes she misses it and the journey continues trying to find her 31.

If we men will cover our women, their journey would only be a trip, and their mistakes would be few while finding her 31. When a woman feels she's running out of time as far as her biological clock goes, she starts doing things not in her nature, like *twerking and jerking in a spasmodic* way, making moves that are sudden at different times in a way that is not in her best interests. Women have a lot of regularity to them: their monthly menstrual cycles, carrying babies nine months before birth, and family time. Women expect men to do regular things as well, like open doors, pay bills on time, date night and cover them. When the regular things are out of order, some women twerk, all because of time. A woman has such a spiritual commitment to bring life into this world that when her horse and carriage (the man) is out of order or in the wrong place, it throws her off -- way off.

Ladies, from now on stop twerking for just anybody and find your 31, because you're grown now; you are no longer a child you're 41 finding your 31. I know you would love to have a mate, but sometimes he's MIA *(missing in action)*. When you're missing, you are just unable to be found at that time; not forever he's out there. He's not dead; just absent. So, what does a woman do to fill that void? Find your 31 and I guarantee you he'll find you, the MIA man would turn to the H-I-A, man, *(here I am)*. Because there's nothing like a juicy steak, with mushrooms cooked to perfection on the grill with a baked potato, butter, sour cream and chives on the side, It's irresistible. Likewise, you will be absolutely irresistible and undeniable to men, when you find your God-given place: your 31.

About the Author

Just like James Brown, the godfather of soul said, "I'm Black and I'm Proud,". I must say this "Lovely" woman you see in this picture with me saved my life (twice). In the book, you will find out how. I grew up in a large family in the projects with lots of love and support from two wonderful parents. But even with all that support, I somehow still found a way to mess that up with riotous living. God had a plan for my life, for some reason...He wouldn't let me die -- HALLELUJAH -- with all those wonderful gifts inside of me. Believe me, I tried many ways of living out of control. When I had had Enough and was ready to throw in the towel, God placed an angel with big wings in my life to lean on. He came to my beauty salon business, that day was kind of slow, so

I started to wonder off. Then suddenly out of nowhere I nodded on and off and the angel watching over me moved its wing, and those wings were all the colors of the Rainbow, 100 times brighter then bright. Then a light in my head came on to let me know God had me covered, and just like that my whole life turned around. Now I see why I couldn't die: I was supposed to tell you in this book that we are to serve God and live on top of the world. I have an amazing story to share with you about Man-Versus- Himself in the form of Woman. So, ladies and gentlemen, if you're ready let's go to that place to where only the butterflies fly.